*REAL LIFE ENCOURAGEMENT
FROM REAL LIFE EXPERIENCES*

WHY SHOULD YOU CARE?

CHARITY PLEASANT

Copyright © 2024 Pleasant Investments LLC Charity Pleasant
All rights reserved
First Edition

Contents

Introduction v
Love, Hate, and Other Things 1
Can We Improve an Imperfect System? 7
I Lived Through a Pandemic 19
Why Aren't You Afraid? 31
Not Everyone is a Believer 41
Why Plant Roots in a Place Only Meant to be Temporary? 45
That Phone Call 51
Shh! Don't Say that! 55
What Are We Really Doing About This? 67
You Again 77
How to Move from Test to Testimony 89
My True Love is Entrepreneurship 95
Life Is But a Dream 101

Introduction

IF YOU THINK that this book is going to be full of cute and cuddly thoughts and words, think again. This is more like a call to action. Maybe the next one will be bushy tails and butterfly flails. As a matter of fact, why don't I start by saying the following words, expressions, and examples that will fill these pages are directly from my thoughts of my experiences. You'll know my style right away if you've read my first book, an autobiography, and will want to finish this one as well.

I also include my observations of the ever-changing world we live in. That means the following words are from my unfiltered opinions and perspectives. I have debated the things that naturally come to my mind when I have time to sit and just think about the events happening in our world. I ask myself so many questions about life, rules, governing authorities, health, money, and the economy. When I ponder the way things are, I answer those questions in a way that makes sense to me. I want to provoke thought and change by expressing what I think others may have rolling around in their minds, too.

If, after you read the words that I'm so proudly sharing with you, no feelings, thoughts, or actions follow on your part, then you're probably not challenging yourself to look through another perspective. To help encourage moving those thoughts from mind to action, I'm sharing these words as my part in the action. I hope that conversations will blossom, groups will thrive, and people will unite in action to improve our beautiful world. In the following pages, I'm challenging you to reconsider your perspective or challenge me to re-think mine.

I've noticed that some of the natural-born rights we all have as citizens are being censored. Like what I choose to put into my body or not. Basic answers to genealogy like male and female that have historically been considered absolute truth are now open to interpretation. I often wonder, does anyone else have that same nudging feeling in the back of their head that something isn't right? It seems that all it takes for something that has been undeniably true to be changed is for a few people to feel otherwise. At that point, the truth is considered subjective.

I think of the laws that were made by our government many years ago that weren't made to include "all" people. The fact is, at the time the Constitution and Bill of Rights were formed, some humans were still considered property. If that stings a little, it should. Even many years after, some of the same laws still exist that don't include everyone. In our government today, laws are created, amended, or removed that not everyone is aware of, even though they benefit some and not others. I often think that our Constitution needs to be rewritten to represent all Americans, to include all people. So why not put a few people in a room again and do just that?

What will it take for us as a nation to exercise our democratic rights? I mean everyone to participate in national, regional, and local elections? I don't omit myself either. I don't always exercise my local voting rights, but I know I should.

The nagging thought in the back of my mind tells me to participate in educational meetings for my son's school such as the PTA, NEA, or NWEA. I should be involved in those groups, associations, or

WHY SHOULD YOU CARE?

meetings as often as I can that greatly affect what is being taught and implemented for our nation's children. I want to be more a part of the process of choosing the topics of what can and cannot be discussed in public schools. I hope that you can see as clearly as I can that sometimes it's like we're the frog in the pot, complacent even as the water is gradually boiling, like the wise metaphor says. Slowly but surely, we're being desensitized to the ever-changing societal norms. Believe me, I don't object to change. I do object to being left out of the critical educational decisions being made on behalf of our children.

I really hope many will realize we cannot afford to see the major issues in our country that need changing and do nothing about it. I recently got an up-close glimpse at how my local election process is managed when I volunteered as a ballot judge in my community. I have to say I was impressed with the people from young to mature who gave their time and talents to help in making the election process as smooth and accurate as possible. But I was surprised by the number of people who needed translators with them in order to cast their votes. I wondered how thoroughly they really understood the information on the ballots as their votes were cast.

There are so many changes happening in our world, both unfamiliar and uncomfortable. With all that is being spotlighted in our news and media, we sometimes forget the pain that we as humans experience through loss, grief, failure, and disappointments. We get used to hearing about fatalities and dishonest people doing unethical things on the daily news programs and timeline feeds. Why is it so hard to believe someone's pain, depression, or feeling of being at the end of their rope? I'm able to have empathy with people by trying to imagine what it would be like to be in their position. Even when it comes to the situations people face, I try and understand how differently people process their realities. Since I know our brains aren't all built the same, my thoughts of what I'd do or how I might react in the same place may differ from someone else's, and realizing this drives me to have more empathy. If I've not experienced it, the magnitude of the reality is incomprehensible. So, the best that I can do is try and understand how one is feeling without judgment. When I see something shocking on my news feed, I often stop and think: there are two sides to every story. I'm not so quick to judge because most of the time I'm only seeing one.

Are all the mantras of motivation leading us to believe one can just pull themselves out of hardships, depression, poverty, or other struggles by the power of positive thinking alone? Mental health in our country is a serious problem all around us, evident by anxiety, fear, depression, withdrawal, mass shootings, suicide, or other acts of violence and atrocities. How long will we ignore the cries for help, crippling people from receiving the aid they so desperately need? Our government spends billions of dollars overseas amid our country's great need. Don't get me wrong, I don't object to funding overseas when necessary. It's just that you don't have to drive far before seeing someone on a corner with a sign asking for help, or others walking the streets, obviously outside of themselves or otherwise affected by drugs or alcohol. So many people cannot afford or do not have medical insurance to help obtain the services they need. If they do, there are some medical insurance premiums that are so high, they still cannot obtain the help they need.

I pass acquaintances all the time walking quickly to an apparent destination while asking me the question, "How are you?" often times without slowing their strides. This leads me to believe they don't have time to hear my response to the question they'd just asked me. It was just a generic question, one with the intent for politeness to be shown by their words. I hope we can slow our strides and show that

WHY SHOULD YOU CARE?

we really want to hear how one is doing more often than not. You never know if listening will lead you to a way of impacting a person's life. I hope that you will ponder some of my questions, thoughts, and realities while I express how I deal with these and other mentally and emotionally challenging topics. You may even relate to the way I put some of my experiences into words. Most importantly, I'm speaking my truth and believe that everyone should have a voice, no matter how big or small. Thus, I'm using mine in the best way I know how…with words.

CHAPTER 1

Love, Hate, and Other Things

IS IT POSSIBLE for love and hate to exist in the same room? Same heart? How about joy and pain? Hope and doubt? One of the things I love about life is all the emotions I feel, absorb, and share. Especially the good ones. When I think about love, I think about a romantic movie, a couple, an expression for a friend or relative, brotherly or sisterly love. Love can be expressed in literally thousands of ways. The dictionary describes it as, "An affection of the mind excited by beauty and worth of any kind, an affection based on admiration, or to hold dear." Love, on so many levels, is benevolent, awe-inspiring, enthusiastic, and warm. When I think about love, I think about my family, my relatives, my God, or the things that ignite and excite my passions.

There are some foods that, when I eat them, send an overwhelming sensory signal from my tongue to my brain. That signal ignites a feeling of love that cascades from my mouth to other parts of me. The feeling causes me to say, "Mmm this is delicious, I love the taste, texture, and smell." There are some restaurants I go to because I simply love the food and service. I enjoy the freshness of the ingredients that outperform other places of business.

Love is comforting. Love causes me to persevere and open my heart time and time again, even after I feel slighted, ignored, or misunderstood by the people closest to me. At times, love has felt conditional, like when I don't give my son exactly what he wants. He tells me I never do anything for him in those moments, even though I know that isn't true. I found that children need to be taught how to love as well as see it in action. They also need to feel unconditional love, too. That's why no matter how many times my son hurts my feelings or disappoints me, I will continue to tell him how much I love him, and there isn't anything that will change my love for him.

Right alongside that love lies hate. I hate that love isn't always enough. I hate that love doesn't always hold together marriages, friendships, or other commitments in some cases. Hate that good nutritional food is so expensive. Hate that life often happens with so much heartache, suffering, and pain. I hate that evil is always present in a world full of love and people doing wonderful things to improve our societies. I hate that truth will always be so subjective. Hate that two people with different beliefs can't focus more on their common attributes. I hate that some Democrats won't be friends with Republicans or vice versa. I hate that right and wrong aren't so simple anymore. Why are there so many gray areas? I think the gray areas are there so that one doesn't have to take a definitive side, such as making a choice to be for or against. I hate that so many are misled with a spin on information to sway the minds of so many intelligent people. I hate that so many must work so many hours to provide for their families. For some, even with an extra job, overtime hours, or bonuses, it's still a struggle for them to eat with skyrocketing food prices. I try not to let things that I cannot control consume such distaste, because I cannot give feelings of hate permanent space in my thoughts or heart. It would be too difficult to focus on love if I did so.

WHY SHOULD YOU CARE?

I have had joy through my pains many times in my life. The joys send me on emotional highs while the pain sends me on emotional lows. One instance where the two were visible in the same room was when I gave birth to my son. Although the pain was great during my labor, the joy that existed during the process was equally as great. Amid the pain, I knew I was birthing something beautiful. The pain I was experiencing was endurable because of the joy of bringing my child into the world. Sometimes while running for exercise my muscles send these pain signals to my brain that make me want to quit. If I don't succumb to the pain, I run my full intended distance. After I finish running my set distance, I feel a little less pain, but the joy of finishing what I started out to accomplish feels even greater. The truth is that life is full of joy. Unfortunately, it's also filled with pain. If you live long enough, you'll experience many of these emotions multiple times over. I prolong the joys as long as I can because I know that pain is inevitable sometime in life.

At times, during the process of working toward a goal, I have both hope and doubt at the same time. I hope that the universe will help align things for me for all my hard work. I hope I have truly done all I can to ensure that all else will fall into place. But in the back of my mind, I sometimes doubt that my goal is even worthwhile, like finishing this book. I hope it is received well. But at times doubt if I should bother to reach and connect with people. I hope my writing is influencing others in a good way. But sometimes, I doubt if I'm good enough, or if my goal is unrealistic. Maybe I'm shooting too high and should leave well enough alone. I recognize these dual feelings, and at times I have to feed the positive vibes to my brain a little more. I have to remind myself to continue challenging myself. I remind myself that sometimes insecurities will show up to tempt me from pushing for what I want to bring to fruition. I only have to continue to believe that anything is possible, any dream can become a reality, and anything worthwhile is worth nurturing and pursuing with tenacity. This helps me to push those doubtful feelings aside to make more room for hope.

My son was about seven months old when his dad and I went on our first date since bringing him home. I both loved the idea of going on a date and hated the idea of leaving my son with a sitter. I remember doing so much research interviewing potential babysitters and asking friends and family for recommendations. I searched newspapers, the Yellow Pages—yes you heard correctly, the Yellow Pages. Remember that giant phone book that weighed a ton? I called daycares only to find that childcare was too expensive. Since my son's father was home after he was born, we only needed occasional sitters when we had outings, commitments, or dates.

We had interviewed a particular lady, and I felt very comfortable with the way she was handling our son and her overall demeanor and experience. So, one day we decided to give her a go. We'd planned something simple for the two of us, dinner and a movie the night we decided to go out. As we were leaving our son with the new sitter, he was crying as he watched us walk out of the door. I thought he was too young to be acutely aware we were leaving him with someone new. She reassured us everything would be okay as I was having second thoughts altogether. But still, off we went to dinner. We sat down, ordered our food, and enjoyed our meal while connecting without interruption. Just as we were finishing our dinner, the sitter called and said our son had not stopped crying since we'd left. She wasn't sure if we'd be okay with that since it had been over an hour since we'd been gone. My heart dropped and I immediately said we'd be right there as soon as we paid our bill. In the background, I could hear our son crying as I told her we'd be back to retrieve him shortly. I don't know how his dad felt, but I couldn't fathom sitting through a movie knowing our son couldn't be consoled. I hated the fact that we left him and regretted it every mile we drew closer to retrieving him. However, I loved the fact that we had given some personal connection with each other a try.

I'm so glad I followed my instincts about the sitter because the mere fact that she called to inform us solidified our good judgment. It cemented that she took great pride in childcare as well as parent care. As we pulled up to her house, I practically jumped out of the car and ran up to the door. To my surprise, there was another person I hadn't met holding my son. I assumed she was a friend or roommate of the sitter, but I was still a bit taken aback. I'll never forget the feeling of seeing the stranger I hadn't even met handing me my son as he sniffed and sobbed himself into restless sleep. That memory hits me so vividly that even today I can re-imagine those memories of our son crying in his sleep. I didn't know how us leaving him would affect him, but when we dropped him off, he must not have been comfortable with her even though he met her previously. Or maybe he was just accustomed to seeing his parents' faces. Some children will go to anybody while others will hold close to those they know. I'd found that out over the years from others who had children before me.

Thinking back on it, I don't know why I would've expected him to be okay after one visit. I'm not sure if he sensed something that I did not that day, but his reaction kept me from going on any other dates, dinner or otherwise, without bringing him along for quite a while. He may've very well had a sixth sense kick in. Either way, after that experience I didn't leave him with anyone but family until he was three years old. Call me a sucker, but I wasn't as brave as many other parents are every day. I figured that by three he could at least somewhat communicate with me about how people treated him. There were those dual feelings again of love and hate existing at the same time. I loved the fact that the sitter had called us but hated that another strange person was trying to console my son.

Now that my son is a teenager, it's much easier to get information from him when I want to know about his days away from home. I love our conversations about how his day was at school, sports practices, and other experiences. I love seeing how his eyes light up when he's sharing something he feels is amusing, even if I don't. I hate that he can always tell when I'm slightly distracted because he asks, "Mom, are you listening?" I try and remind myself to listen diligently and make sure I'm giving responses at the appropriate times and give the appropriate reactions that show I'm engaged. I love that my son is growing and maturing into his own person. I just hate to see it happening so quickly. It both pains me and gives me joy to see he doesn't need me to be so hands-on with him anymore because I'm raising him to be independent. I often doubt that he will need me to guide him as much in the future because he's doing so well on his own, but I still hope he does. I hope that I'll never regret being the woman who helps him become the man he will be. I doubt that the man he is sure to become will disappoint me. So, yes. Love and hate, joy and pain, hope and doubt can exist at the same time, in the same room, or even in the same heart. I'm living proof of that.

CHAPTER 2

Can We Improve an Imperfect System?

MURDER, ADDICTION, LYING, cheating, stealing, selfishness, foolishness, ignorance, hatred, and spitefulness all equals sin. Imperfection started all the way back with Adam. Some would say it was because of Adam. Others blame Eve. Some say, "Why didn't God only punish one or both of them?" I know I do. I thought one time, why didn't he get rid of them both and start humans all over again with only the will to do, "good?" I believe that it's because God wanted mankind to have a choice through human nature. I don't believe God has ever wanted to force man to serve him. I won't go into the details from the Garden of Eden, so if you don't know the story, look it up in the book of Genesis in the Bible. From what I observe in my daily life, many systems and humanity are going in the wrong direction at an alarming rate in my opinion. That doesn't encompass all systems and humankind. There are some systems that are working really well. There are also people who are spearheading a lot of good providing solutions to problems in our world. Can we make improvements?

There are some activists doing some great work to bring awareness, improvement, and change like Reverend Al Sharpton, Bill and

Melinda Gates, Michelle Obama, and many other non-industry names that most people don't even know about. Such as Audre Lorde, a former activist or Robert Hillary King, who advocated against solitary confinement. There are so many people worth talking about who don't get nearly the same national coverage as a messy Hollywood divorce, which used to dominate the entertainment magazines covers, not the news outlets. People less known are depending on far more independent sources like NPR or XM radio, podcasts, flyers, meetings, or other streaming services to reach listeners.

Some of our trusted news stations and outlets that we've depended on for truthful and reliable information no longer are satisfied with reporting actual news alone. It seems they've jumped on board with more social aspects of society of what sells instead of the meaty subjects of our livelihood. Take for example, changes in Roe vs. Wade or other political matters and laws being altered that are changing our lives and societies. There isn't as much coverage of the stories that spread ways we can enact real change in our government. I've noticed that some media sources wait until the end of the program to briefly highlight one feel-good story. The rest often seem really negative or sad to me.

It seems at times the people behind the news whether it be the donors, writers, station CFO, CEO, or whomever, prefer to manipulate stories. For example, they show angles of stories that cause people to perceive it in ways that seem to justify why we're being convinced to accept new ideas or vaccines. Think about this: a renowned doctor pleads with people on television to take a vaccine. My thoughts go to, *There must be someone who counts on this doctor to sway much of the public into following suit because of the trust in a said doctor held by the public.* Another example is of a doctor talking on the news coverage outlets about taking a pill to lower cholesterol. The person's statement can hold an authoritative weight so people will look to pills instead of changing their eating habits and exercising to lower their numbers. I often ask myself why an actor's or actress's affair makes the news in the first place. Is it a distraction from what is truly happening in our world of importance? We all know gossip sells. I just don't believe gossip should be news. I'd rather hear from an investigative journalist about a piece they've been working on.

Meanwhile, there are people improving technology and adding modern conveniences right in front of us that should make the top story. But the negative story continues to put a blanket over our eyes to the real life-changing matters that affect our daily choices right now.

Once we realize the real breakdown that is being done in our society—and I'm hoping we wake up and see it—most of the damage that has occurred will take years or lifetimes to undo. Take our environment, for example. I hope I'm not the only one who's still trying to make heads or tails of global warming.

You only have to look at the state of our children killing each other or themselves, stealing cars, adults being locked up by the thousands, or human trafficking or other brutalities to be concerned of what is being done about them. Families are being severed from the instrumental foundation that is needed in our communities. So many people have to pay the price of inflation, economic disadvantage, and other loss of freedoms and securities. It's imperative not just now but in the future as well that we all unite for the positive changes that we want to see in how our country improves societal needs in a way that impowers people to improve themselves.

When I think about the laws that are changed to put specific people at a disadvantage, I'm disheartened. The ones that make it harder for all people to vote. The ones that allow taxes to cover abortion costs. If a person wants or needs to have an abortion, that's their choice. But I don't believe tax dollars or government spending should help pay for it, the person wanting the procedure should be responsible.

The law enforces me to renew my driver's license every year, even though nothing has changed since my last visit. This makes me feel taken advantage of. All that money and time spent at the DMV with a clerk that may or may not be personable, only to emerge with a sticker for my troubles. I must admit I get a little upset at the money and time I spend that could've been used somewhere else. Why has this law not been changed over the years to space out the renewal period? Why not only renew when I move or make a new car purchase? Maybe updated to every five-year renewal period at a lower cost, to say the least.

The information super-highway—the internet—has been a vehicle for us to spread a message, and we should be spreading a powerfully positive one. Even before the internet, there were all sorts of morally wrong things I mentioned above lurking in our world. Now, we're not only more aware of them instantly because of the World Wide Web, but anyone can spread those negative threads many times at lightning speed, as well as spread misinformation. Millions of people knowingly or unknowingly spread hurtful messages that they shouldn't with the click of one finger. They spread rumors and click like or share buttons to further push comments throughout the social universe. I remember my mother telling me when I was young, "If you don't have anything nice to say, don't say nothing at all." We could all use a mantra now that starts, "If you don't have anything nice to spread..." You get the rest, right?

WHY SHOULD YOU CARE?

People using their phones during special dinners hurt real meaningful conversations. I've seen people with their phones under the table during work meetings, classes, and behind the wheel of a car throughout the day. How much more focused could people be if they were simply turned off during these times? Have our phones really taken control of our entire lives? Have the need-to-know trending topics, news, and how many likes caused us to be addicted to how much we *"think"* we know? These small handheld devices demand our attention with every ping, every light-up, and every vibration.

I feel some advancements in technology have been both a blessing and a distraction. These same technologies improve our lives in so many ways, like reaching our families quicker and more easily. They are useful also for keeping track of them and being able to stay in touch with family members that are far away. But how do we minimize the harm and amplify the good? My answer would involve the family. It takes the foundation that families lay for one another and their children to help strengthen and enhance our societies. I believe that the rules, boundaries, love, and support will help communities of people to work hand in hand. It will take no cell phone rules during meals to encourage conversations. Maybe even locking out Wi-Fi after 11 p.m. to ensure you, your partner, or your child isn't up all night on their phone or other electronic devices. It may even take other extra steps like parental controls on your child's devices.

I look at several social media outlets, and when I don't like what's being said or shown, I no longer participate in that thread. It's super easy to do. Why do people constantly back-peddle their words, thoughts, and feelings to appease other people? Some often retract statements or apologize for what they said not because they're sorry but because of loss of endorsements, followers, public opinion, and other repercussions. In actuality, we have all said or done something that we've regretted. Fortunately, in life, we grow if we're lucky. We evolve from who we used to be to who we are. Some people can't help but remind us of who we used to be. The truth often is hard to swallow because it demands action. Why are things taken so personally? When did the First Amendment lose so much of its value? We all have freedom of speech here in America:

> "Congress shall make no law respecting an establishment of religion, or prohibiting the free exercise thereof; or abridging the freedom of speech, or of the press; or the right of the people peaceably to assemble, and to petition the Government for a redress of grievances." (Library of Congress)

We seem to live in a time when it is popular to try and ruin someone over something you don't agree with. How did we get to the place where stating what you believe is so offensive? I have been hearing about more lawsuits recently than I've ever heard in previous years. My mom used to hurt my feelings quite a bit with her responses and directives. I think in a way that helped me not to be so sensitive to others who could've easily offended me. I was already versed in communication dynamics in many different settings. What my mother often conveyed is that as the adult, she was the authority figure. Such huge deals are made when people's feelings are hurt these days. When I was growing up, I learned that most of the negative connotations voiced were from people who didn't understand how powerful their words could be. As an adult, I found some people are just mean.

I saw a news story once about a couple that complained that a local business establishment refused to make them a cake because of their belief against a certain lifestyle. Why would anyone want to be serviced by a person or business who doesn't wish to service them? I wouldn't trust that the product or service would be superior. There are thousands of bakeries in operation. If a business refuses to serve me based on race, gender, or other origins, I wouldn't want to knowingly force them to service me. I would, however, want their practices to change in fairness to all people. Why would I give them my business knowing it wouldn't be done out of passion, care, and love? I would take my business and money somewhere else. I don't see a need to drive national attention to the circumstance because of it. I'm not ignorant to knowing that people are imperfect. Inconsistencies as well as inequalities still exist and need to be improved. Yes, I hope that we will get closer to shortening the gap between them, but I'm not surprised they still happen.

When did we get to the point where it's much easier for us to hate than it is to love? One of the reasons I share my writing is because I love people. I love to experience culture, new foods, new places, and new ideas. I have always thought outside the box because I have never fit inside one. As an adult, I do believe we should be open to others' viewpoints in a judgment-free zone. Not all of them need to be open to interpretation. But I also believe other people should be open to me disagreeing or refusing to support some of their views. There is seldom a time where I hear or know of any two people that agree on everything but still have great relationships. Even with the difference of views, it might be possible to find other things to agree on. That doesn't mean a person can't be friendly. I can and will still respect others' perspectives, treat them kindly, and wish more people could do the same.

I see constant hints of tolerance to this or that has been etched into commercials, schools, kids' and adult televisions shows, advertisements, news outlets—to name a few. When I dive into the word tolerance, I often ask myself, "Do children or adults need to be more tolerant?" Often times I believe it's the adults. One way tolerance is defined is by showing willingness to allow the existence of opinions and behavior one may not necessarily agree with. Most of the children I've connected with over the years have a natural ability to be unbiased to others. Of course there's always the exception. It makes me think there is an agenda to tell children how to think as early as possible. When I was growing up, it was the parents job to guide a child's mind.

I took my son to an animated movie recently in which the scene was set up that a same-sex couples had a baby. There was no explanation behind on how this couple achieved it since it couldn't happen organically, but I thought about how it could confuse a young child watching. When will we get tired and say, "that's enough"? I believe a children's movie should be free of all innuendos.

I personally don't believe children need to understand sex in kindergarten. I would want my child to be focused on a list of parent approved subjects in elementary school. He's finishing middle school now and I still don't want him to be privy to what other people's sexual orientations are. That's their business, not his. Mainly it shouldn't matter because we are all people, however we describe ourselves. I prefer him to focus on Math, English, History, Science, and the Arts. I believe elementary and secondary education is so important to lay the foundational groundwork to our children's educational understanding.

I don't believe that politicians or governments alone should decide how our children are educated. I want to choose when and how my child is exposed to important topics, to learn about them in my home first and not his school. I have the right to control what my child is exposed to and subjected to when inside a state or federally funded institution. After all, I pay taxes. It seems subject matters outside

WHY SHOULD YOU CARE?

the traditional educational curriculum appear to be high on agendas, which is puzzling to me. I'm guessing most people have become too busy, or just don't care, to stay informed on how much our education system has changed. I do believe there is a time and place for those who want to promote more open subjects to kids, and they should be provided with a safe space outside of public schools to do so, like a recreation center or club.

When I think about the way our educational system is managed today, I cringe. It's not just what is being discussed but what's not. Our history is important and should be relevant, but why do we spend so much time on the past? Education should be more focused on preparing for what's ahead in the future, instead of memorizing past events, in my opinion. Everyone needs to understand where America has made mistakes in the past in order to pave a brighter future. Thankfully we live during a time of modern advances that help people move further and faster with newer technology. The advancements should be used more frequently to create more alternative learning styles. More students would want to engage if they didn't have to sit so still at a desk most of the day. It's a huge disservice that some of our youth won't be prepared to excel and succeed in the workforce and life.

Financial literacy is what should be a huge focus in our school system from kindergarten onward. Don't believe me? All you have to do is look at the astronomical debts that our country is in. I literally cannot fathom what will happen when I grow older and need this generation to assume financial care and welfare for me. Aside from the massive government debt, there are more consumers than ever with overwhelming credit card debts, college loans, and medical debt. How will education prevent the future generations from repeating the cycle? Participation in decisions is a must if we are to teach the future generation discipline, responsibility, and consequences. Money and how to properly manage it should be taught as early as possible to help cement responsible stewardship.

Have you heard the increase of things that children are saying they will and won't do to adults? I don't have to be in a grocery store long these days without hearing a child telling their parent no. I wonder sometimes how some of the youth of today will hold down a job without the proper preparation they need to excel and succeed. It's a huge disservice. They lack the ability to respect those who are guardians over them now. I've seen firsthand that children are making decisions they're way too young to be making. Children's brains aren't developed enough to make the critical decisions they're being allowed to make. It's our fault. An environment has been created that has allowed them to do so. They stopped hearing the word, "no." I tell people sometimes, "No is not a bad word." You can say no sometimes because kids need some limitations in their lives. Adults need them too. There should be boundaries and mutual respect between children and adults. Unfortunately, that rarely exists in the circles I travel today. It's not too late to teach the future generations how they can be more respectable citizens. There are thousands, if not more, resources available in almost every format imaginable, covering any topic if one may need a bit of guidance. I wouldn't want our children accepting the status quo. I want them to far exceed what is asked of them. It's not a question; we must improve our educational system. Too many other societal balances rely on the outcome.

Does anyone know when prayer was taken out of school? Approximately 1962. Has the education environment gotten better or worse since that change? I'll let you answer that. But while you ponder, how many mass shootings in school were there prior to 1962? I remember my K-4 teachers praying in front of my class each day before the school day began in my Christian school. Prayer changes things. That was proven on the football field on January 2nd, 2023, during a seemingly ordinary Monday night football game. I witnessed more people praying that night in unity than I had ever seen in my life. Even commentators were praying live on-air for one purpose with most of the millions that were watching. Even onlookers who may've not believed in God or prayer stayed respectfully silent.

Does it not say on every paper dollar, "In God we trust"? Then why don't we place trust in God? We are a nation built on Christian faith. It's time for us to analyze how we can start righting the things that don't add up. We're overdue in thinking about why we don't include God in decision making. If we do not, then maybe we should rethink the message printed on our money, stamped on plaques hanging around various places, and on governing documents. I believe it's imperative that I pray for our leaders, others, and my child. I'm not attempting to make you religious—I promise I'm not. But do you not see the hypocrisy of it all? It's like reading a company mission statement and realizing that it doesn't match what they do. I just want you to think about the nature of issues in our world and how we could move forward effectively.

Isn't it ironic that we place such high values on the ideals and principles our country was built on, but we often don't practice them? One way irony is defined is, "The expression of one's meaning by using language that normally signifies the opposite, typically for humorous or emphatic effect." I don't find the humor of claiming to be a nation built on Christianity but that doesn't, in a large part, practice its principles. I find it ironic that the things that some people around me place value in, I see no value, intrinsic or otherwise. The flip side is that things I find value in, others can care less about. I care a huge deal about the laws in our country, the education system, media outlets, and other systems in place in our world. With everything happening in our world, the best I can do is have a positive impact on what I can impact. Like this book, for example. I hope that I will be able to say that I have changed the trajectory of someone's future because I cared enough to share my words.

So take a minute to ask yourself, where can I be a part of improving the systems in place in our society? Get into the habit of developing and implementing solutions and not just highlighting the problems. We have the chance to set an example that we can share with the future trailblazers of our generations. Our world will never be perfect in any way, shape, or form, but don't let it be from lack of trying. Just remember, throughout history it has taken innovators many failures before seeing success in their projects. Consider the lightbulb by Thomas Edison, electricity credited to Alessandro Volta, or Karl Benz for the automobile. Can you imagine a world if any of these innovators had stopped after the second or any number of times they failed? It took the men involved in drafting the Constitution many days to negotiate and agree on what the final draft would look like. Wherever life's path may take you, remember the roads will be rough at times. You may even take a wrong turn. But you cannot afford to not make it right. Humankind depends on each and every one of us to contribute whatever talent or passion we have to improve an imperfect system.

CHAPTER 3

I Lived Through a Pandemic

I WOULD NOT have imagined in all my life that I would be living in a time that is as comparable to the Bubonic Plague of the 1300s. Not in the effect that we saw—the numbers hit hundreds of millions in death toll—but in effect that the Covid virus was spread worldwide so rapidly. The number of Covid-related deaths being reported worldwide was astonishing, to say the least.

When the Covid virus first hit the mainstream in March of 2020 here in Ohio, I thought for sure it wouldn't cause many disruptions. I hadn't even heard of the virus before then. It was around this time I first noticed the word "Covid" on a Lysol can. Because of researching flu statistics, I thought Covid wouldn't be that concerning. After all, according to the CDC, an estimated 41 million had flu-related illnesses the year of 2017-2018 season. Of those numbers, 50,000+ people died from the complications coupled with the flu illness. (https://www.cdc.gov/flu/about/burden/2017-2018.htm)

I vividly remember standing in the eighth-grade social studies classroom of my job, watching CNN 10 announce the alarming data of COVID-19 infection rates. Students were worried that school would be canceled if the data showed increases in the number of affected persons. I remember telling a few students who were discussing the possibilities, "You all have no need to worry, I doubt if school will be canceled indefinitely." Those were the words I used to try and ease the minds of our students. I was attempting to encourage them to let the adults do the worrying and figure out what was next so they could focus on school tasks. Boy was I wrong.

It wasn't a day or two later that I got the email from my employer saying that school would be mandated to shut down indefinitely. Our government had given instruction for everyone to isolate. Just like that, we were helping students clean out their lockers and sift through what materials would be important to take home. It was so sad to see our students cleaning out their lockers while hugging each other with their goodbyes for now.

Once the building was clear of students, staff had the next day or two to gather our belongings, teaching materials, get out of the building, and prepare to communicate with our students online. It was all hands on deck. Everyone was furiously overworking the copy machines, staplers, hole punchers, putting take-home packets together, assigning loaner Chromebooks to students by number, and so many other tasks to prepare students to learn remotely for the first time. We were all going home without a return date in sight. The entire staff was amazing at pitching in and organizing the pickup plans for students to get their learning materials. With just one announcement, our routine as I knew it had changed.

At that time, I couldn't fathom the effect of all children abruptly being told to stay in the house on such short notice. Also, how would parents be able to work efficiently with their children being home all day? I didn't even consider that adults in every non-essential arena would be told to stay at home as well. How can I not mention the

WHY SHOULD YOU CARE?

essential workers who, amid all of this uncertainty, went into overtime mode to serve the overwhelming need of many people during this time? They were unselfish, leaving their children, families, and livelihoods daily to put themselves at risk for their communities. Who could imagine how this would work out? I know I couldn't.

Once all the staff were at an acceptable level of preparedness, thanks to everyone pitching in to help one another, off to our cars we went. I could not predict what the next few weeks would look like. I only knew my world was flipped upside down.

I slept in a little longer than normal on the days following my exodus. Each day I rose in time to join Zoom meetings, virtual classroom groups, and help my students stay up to date with their online class assignments. One positive result of being at home was being able to eliminate driving time and save on gas for the car.

As the days continued, there were staff Zoom meetings, professional development classes required, and other mental health check-ins occurred. I became an IT person of sorts, trying to help students troubleshoot their cameras, Wi-Fi issues, microphones, audio, and such to keep their learning going. I repeatedly sent personal chats to students to turn cameras back on or mute themselves. I helped with the morale of our students by joining in making entertaining videos by staff for our kiddos to enjoy. Those Zoom classes proved to be a little more difficult than the traditional classroom setting for me. It seemed way more challenging to engage middle school students' attention for very long with their families close in the background carrying on with life.

I willingly took advantage of the extra time this Covid virus had extended to me by cleaning my house from top to bottom. By cleaning I mean taking all the canned goods out of cabinets to wipe down and reorganize, moving couches from against the wall to vacuum and clean behind them, removing couch cushions to vacuum underneath. Taking up mattresses and flipping them after cleaning underneath them, shampooing all my carpet, and these were just a few of my cleaning tasks inside. I cleaned out air ducts and vents, dusted bookshelves, sanitized doorknobs and light switches, too. When I looked around and came to the conclusion that no spot was left untouched, I realized it was only May and I would have the entire summer off from work. To my delight, I had finished all my inside tasks while working online.

So, off to the outside of the house I went. I pulled weeds for days, cut grass, trimmed bushes, and whatever else I could do to spruce up the outside. Once I'd finished, I just kind of looked around satisfied with myself. I took a couple of days to relax and take in the results from all my labors. Suddenly, all the free time wasn't looking as appealing as I originally thought it would be.

Considering I was mostly confined to the house with almost every non-essential business closed. Where could I go for my occasional, sporadic outings? I'm the type of person who enjoys a schedule with a routine and staying occupied with substantial things. Before the mandated stay-at-home order, I had explored new places around the city. Staying home was difficult for me since I also was used to getting up and spontaneously going somewhere new to listen to live music, an open mic event, eat somewhere new, or experience a new activity. I was not at all used to these limitations. It was not a good feeling even though it seemed initially for the good of all.

With non-essential businesses being closed, the summer of 2020 left me homebound after accomplishing all my summer duties in the spring. This had me wondering what I would do to stay busy and productive for the next unforeseeable months ahead. I still didn't know if I had to be back in my building for school in August.

It wasn't long before I eventually exhausted all the shows I wanted to catch up on via Netflix, Prime, and Hulu. I had been taking daily walks or runs to get fresh air in my neighborhood park since the shutdown began. Although the fresh air and exercise were beneficial, it was the same scenery repeatedly. I could only go to the grocery store so many times in a week, just to get out of the house. An upside, if one could say there was one, is that during these months of seclusion, I realized how grateful I was for all I had in life. I was thankful I hadn't contracted the virus. The time I had to catch up, refresh, refocus, and so on somehow felt more valuable. I realized how much I needed to take care of myself mentally and physically and appreciated my family and life on a much higher level of gratitude because of this pandemic.

While others were suffering greatly, I was blessed to be able to continue to pay my bills, not worry about job security, and stay in great mental and physical health. I got to focus on things that were important to me; I wouldn't have had the time to focus on them during a normal work week. I began to sleep well, I continued to drink plenty of water, I talked to and texted to check on my friends and family. I bonded with my son by doing various activities to keep him occupied, I read my Bible and prayed daily, and so many other things that calmed and replenished my spirit. I even finished my manuscript and was ready to publish my first book, an autobiography titled, *All The Things That Nobody Told Me: Finding the Extraordinary in My Journey*, shortly after the pandemic. There were some extraordinary circumstances going on in the world at the time. It seemed the world all around me was in complete shambles.

There were some who were suffering because of the mandate that took away the freedom to conduct business. I understand why so many pushed back against this executive order. It kept millions of people from providing for their families. There are so many roadblocks already that keep thousands of people from even starting their businesses because of the ridiculous fees and hoops you have to jump through to begin with. Many have persevered only to have their businesses snatched away during the mandated lockdown of 2020. Without being able to conduct business, many had no cash flow to pay leases and other related business expenses.

College education is so expensive, and if you're one of the lucky ones that can go, you may end up in an unrelated field or in student loan debt for many years after you complete your degree. As beneficial as the college experience is, it should be more affordable for all to attend. Thousands of people depend on their degrees to earn a living. Then in 2020 so many were kept from using those degrees.

Unfortunately, during the peak of the pandemic, I also witnessed so much division on different mandates happening all around me. It seemed we were a country divided among wearing or not wearing a mask, and then later receiving or not receiving a vaccine. There seemed to be part of the population living on the extreme side with fears of catching Covid and how it may result in health complications or death. This group seemed to have followed the health ordinances precisely. While the other parts preferred to be completely oblivious to all the data or didn't believe the reports at all. This group focused more so on their civil liberties. During this time, they continued to have large gatherings or parties, continued to travel, and chose not to mask while doing so. Many others fell somewhere in between, siding with caution.

WHY SHOULD YOU CARE?

Later during the pandemic, I was at the grocery store and observed from time-to-time some shoppers refusing to wear masks in stores upon request. Patience was thin seemingly everywhere, and who could forget the toilet paper and paper towel shortage? I felt that I fell somewhere in between the scale because while I knew the virus was serious, and took certain precautions, I also knew that I didn't want to stop living my life because of it. I was sure to use my best judgment when it came to how I would protect myself, my son, and others. Agree or disagree, I'm sure many others did what they felt was best for them. It was eye-opening to see how divided people everywhere were on this topic. It lead me to think about all the other topics we as people disagree on. How can we respectfully deal with one another anyway? Are we able to thrive among such divisions? I believe humanity is continuing to answer those questions.

I had begun to feel the effects of the COVID-19 in June when my travel plans got canceled, and utility bills were steadily increasing with my son and I being home all day instead of work and school. That meant I had to find a way to pay the usage jumps without an increase in my salary. Before the virus, I hadn't had internet services at my house and because of moving to online school and work in March, I had to add that expense as well. I needed it for both myself to continue working and for my son not to fall behind in his new online education.

For some reason, food magically started disappearing from the fridge and cabinets at an alarming rate. Just kidding! We ate more frequently being home all day too. As I look back, I realize that though all these additional expenses occurred without a pay raise, I must give honor to God for keeping me during those uncertain times. I cannot fathom the added stress this put on many people's day-to-day lives who were already struggling to make ends meet. I only had to adjust for a family of two. My expenses were only marginal compared to what larger families must've been experiencing.

This may look similar to what a lot of other people were experiencing through the pandemic, or it may not. But I thought to myself at the time, "I have my faith to see me through, what about so many others without faith?" I couldn't imagine how different things would look for me without my faith. My faith allowed me to put my trust in God regardless of the data from the media that seemed to be purposefully inducing fear multiple times per day. I kept thinking of a Bible verse that states, "God hath not given us the spirit of fear but of power and love and a sound mind." (II Timothy 1:7) I prayed for others who were losing family members and friends to the virus. Innumerable people had my sympathy during this period. My heart went out to so many people losing jobs, homes, businesses, and financial security. But I held close to that Bible verse and several others throughout that unforgettable season.

Amid all that was occurring all around the globe, school started back that August online. A few months later hybrid style learning began. Hybrid learning was so different; staff were only interacting with fifty percent of our student population in attendance each day. This decision helped to distance students in the classroom and throughout the building. At the time, I felt that I should be prepared for the uncertainty to continue. More than ever, I wanted to be on guard about the possibilities that could lie ahead. Possibilities like another government ordered shutdown or what I would have in place for income loss, for example. It makes me work harder towards building up financial safety nets and human relationships.

Would things ever go back to normal? I had a feeling that our new normal would look different than it did pre-Covid. I thought to

WHY SHOULD YOU CARE?

myself, what is normal anyway? At any moment, our world could shatter, shake, or be turned upside down. Life can be affected by tragedy or war among other things. At times, our lives change for the better. Maybe a promotion, a winning lottery ticket, a surprise pregnancy, or a college degree. I wondered if this Covid experience would help us to permanently change our routines for the betterment of all? Or would it soon be back to business as usual after things settle down? Only time could tell. My hope is that all of us who lived to see the other side of this pandemic will cherish more, realize who or what is important in life, and learn to work together in our homes and communities.

I hope this experience will be more than just a thing of the past. At the height of so many problems we tend to be on guard and unite for a common purpose. Then with time we so easily forget what we've just gone through and how we worked together to accomplish amazing goals. We will certainly have some growing pains and adjustments to make both in our professional and personal lives. Who knows the lasting effects COVID-19 will still have on our world in the future? What will future history books say about this time period? I know one thing: the lines are longer in the grocery stores, fast food lanes, drive-thru teller machines, and many other service industries. Shipping shortages, product outages, lean staffing, and furloughs are just a few of the burdens we all are living with. During those long waits, I try to remember to be grateful that someone showed up for work, albeit waiting in long lines. I'm thankful that I have money to pay for the items I need. So, I try hard not to complain that customer service isn't speedy anymore. Although I must admit, I'm not 100 percent at it yet. I try to remember this experience may've soured some people's general outlook on our government, politicians, their own families or friends, and life. Others will be permanently scarred from this experience. It will be hard not to be after one remembers how they were treated for whatever stance they took or the decisions that they made during this time. Whenever new struggles and tough times occur in the future, I hope that we remember the empathy, compassion, and patience we showed each other throughout this unprecedented experience.

I heard the President say recently that our economy is stronger than ever. I've also heard it said that truth is subjective, but how far can that be taken? When I visit the grocery stores, I see firsthand how the prices have increased 20, 30, or 35 percent on most of the items I have bought repeatedly. Along with the price increase came a decrease in the size of some of the containers. It's obvious to me that the President or politicians who claim the economy is doing great don't do the family grocery shopping or can afford not to look at the bill. There is no other way to see situations like this except as they are. We only need to talk to a neighbor, family member, or friend who has lost a job, business, or livelihood in a short amount of time to see how the economy is.

With the likelihood of these adversities continuing, I'm doing several things to plan for the shifts in our economy and would recommend my readers to try to do one or two things as well. I'm attempting to save a little extra money, I buy a little extra non-perishables at the grocery store each week, I try to eliminate some unnecessary spending, I work on ways to create a secondary income, and just being aware that life can change in an instant. You may be doing a few of the same things or something totally different, like getting involved with politics and campaigns in your community. Or maybe you're starting a community garden, collecting reusable items to give away, or gathering signatures to petition for the changes you want to see. The main idea is to do something in preparation for things we can't always control but hope to improve. We must all play our part in what we are passionate about. I'm convinced that if we all take our sections of the bigger parts then all will be improved for the better. I heard a quote recently that said, "Motivation can fade in an instant, inspiration can last as long as you stay inspired." Whenever life begins to feel overwhelming, and believe me it will, I remember that I've lived through a pandemic. You share the same victory because you are reading these words. Because we survived to see the other side of this worldwide virus, let's not waste a minute. We beat the odds. So, let's take whatever inspiration as far as we can with the gratitude of surviving a pandemic.

CHAPTER 4

Why Aren't You Afraid?

FEAR, ACCORDING TO the dictionary, is painful agitation in the presence or anticipation of danger. There are many reasons to be afraid. The first thing that I'm afraid of are food dangers. This fear occurs because I'm aware of many of the ways foods are grown and processed in the US. I'm aware because of the many food documentaries I watch, the articles I read in print, and simply by seeing and tasting how different foods are now compared to my childhood.

Are you afraid of the food in your kitchen cabinets, refrigerators, or freezers? You should be; they could be filled with pesticides, herbicides, additives, and Lord knows what else. The meat in your refrigerators can include growth hormones, herbicides, pesticides, plumped with water, and many other undesirable ingredients. Some common active ingredients in chemical herbicides include glyphosate, atrazine, dicamba, paraquat, triazine, diquat, glufosinate, metolachlor, urea derivatives, trifluralin, and/or surfactants. Pesticides can include: acephate, bendiocarb, bifenthrin, boric acid, capsaicin, carbaryl, chlorantraniliprole, and/or chlordane. Now, I had to look most of those terms up to understand what they were. Above are just some of the chemical ingredients that could be lurking in US food supply. To think that all these unnatural and harmful ingredients could be sprayed onto crops, seeping into the soil, and seeping into our bodies. Does that sound natural? I think it sounds scary.

I want to demand from the rooftop that our food regulators put a stop to these things in our food supply. It should be a crime for massive corporations to monopolize the food supply. I can't be the only one to see documentaries of farmers being cut off from their livelihoods in ways that make it impossible to grow and harvest foods ethically. It seems they're being bullied into buying hybridized seeds and using feed supplied by large companies who even tell the farmers how to grow their own animals or else they won't buy them. I'm doing what I can by purchasing organic when possible, growing some vegetables myself without crop spraying, and buying from local farmers markets. I fear that I and a few others like me alone won't be enough to help farmers sustain clean and healthy food chains or maintain their farm and way of making a living. Buying organic can get very expensive when it should be a natural human right. I'm afraid of how hard my body will have to work to keep up with detoxifying so many harmful substances. That's why I do my best to eat as clean as possible.

There's no secret that people love to consume food, myself included. But have you noticed that we're constantly consuming mantras of "do whatever makes you feel good." This is not a good idea to encourage for many reasons. Often people lose control when in the moment enjoying themselves. Some people enjoy harming others. Others enjoy what may be considered inappropriate to some. If we all ate whatever made us feel good, many of us would be overweight and unhealthy. If ice cream made your child feel good and they ate it three meals per day, it wouldn't end with great results. Do you see just how easily doing what you feel can be taken too far? The thing about a feeling is it's temporary and will need to be repeated to regain

WHY SHOULD YOU CARE?

the initial satisfaction. That's why I cannot understand the do-what-feels-good mantra.

As a result of all the unhealthy things being put into the US food market, there is a health crisis of many illnesses affecting our quality of life. Why aren't more people looking into cures for ailments that can be obtained by changing the way we eat or grow our food? Regular, consistent exercise along with a personalized diet can eliminate some health irregularities. I've seen documentaries and testimonials that have proved healthy changes can help. Are you not afraid that our FDA has less-than-desirable food regulations? The standards just aren't high enough for me. Regulations that allow big companies to dominate the food industry with subpar growing ingredients and methods that speed and plump up growth. So many animals are grain fed in less-than-ideal living environments, instead of being grassfed and pasture raised. The size of the chicken legs, thighs, and breasts, I see in stores today are three times the size they were in my childhood. Wouldn't you like to stop eating the food that is slowly deteriorating your health and demand that food supply is humanely sourced? I strongly believe we must find a way to stop shopping in ways that break down our immune systems so badly and get closer to nature. When I say nature, I don't mean we should all become farmers. I mean having a clear conscience when choosing the food we buy, eating more fresh food and less processed ones.

Thank goodness that there are people like Rachel Parent advocating for food transparency and proper labeling of genetically engineered foods. She and others are passionate about giving Americans choices of what impacts our bodies by the ingredients that we put into them. Rachel advocates for more teaching healthy growth and labeling practices. She supports natural food growers and harvesters who ensures that healthy food is readily labeled, accessible and affordable for all. I think about places like Italy that do not allow for high levels of harmful pesticides, herbicides, or other chemicals to be put into the crops and growing processes. Boy! I'd like to live there in a place where I wouldn't have to worry as much about my food choices because standards didn't allow inhumane processes within agricultural methods.

My second fear is the healthcare system. Medicine has become a huge monetary business. It's no big secret that up until the 1900s most of modern medicine was holistic in nature, homeopathic, naturopathic, and herbal practice. Those were almost all that were commonly used. I cannot say that those methods healed people 100 percent of the time, only that there are many studies of cases that have shown these non-traditional methods can be effective. Pharmaceutical companies reap the most benefits with their multi-million-dollar earnings. I can't figure out why the drugs people so desperately need cost so much. Greed is the only thing I can come up with. The Flexner Report that was commissioned by Andrew Carnegie shares about a group of people who evaluated the medical schools and institutions. The result of the report alarmed people, and funding ended for those schools and institutions in the arenas I mentioned above, resulting in the closures of non-traditional practices all over the US. You can guess who benefited monetarily from this report. A lot of the above holistic practices have been moving back into mainstream in terms of popularity and usefulness.

There have actually been pharmaceutical representatives in my doctor's office when I've had an appointment telling my doctor of this or that new drug to "try" on patients. One pharmaceutical rep even looked directly at me and said to my doctor, "Maybe you can try this new drug on her? She looks like she meets the parameters." I looked straight at the rep and said, "No way, I'm certainly not a good candidate for your experiment."

In my eyes, new drugs are just that, an experiment. Its effects aren't known until a wide enough group of people have taken them and data can be drawn. I can't bring myself to overlook many of the side effects to decide whether it's even worth the medication. I'm a fan of getting to the root of the problem and correcting it, not taking a pill to control it. I know that's not always possible, and that's where modern medicine comes in handy and is effective. It is my opinion that doctors are trained to treat symptoms, not the causes. So, I have to look at the whole system and how it's designed to make choices with my health. I am a fan of holistic healing and appreciate the advances that modern medicine has to offer. But I still do my research on what I can naturally do to improve my health and wellbeing.

Every so often my third fear—the unknown—shows up. For some, the unknown can be quite stressful. When I was a little girl, probably around age eight or nine, my sister and I were in the bathroom early one morning, I was still half asleep. We must've been getting ready for school or church. The next thing I knew, my sister started screaming and turned to run out of the bathroom. Alerted by her scream and seeing her about to run out, I quickly grabbed her white t-shirt (hanging by her coattail, per se) and held on for dear life as I tried to keep up. Her legs were longer than mine. As I was fleeing the bathroom with her, trying to keep up with her pace, her shirt was ripping in my tight grip as we ran down the hallway. The reason I grabbed her shirt was because I thought there was some type of danger I wasn't unaware of. Her scream led me to believe that I should be afraid too. You see, I wasn't about to be left behind by myself, knowing that something frightened her enough to make her scream and run. I had no idea what it was, but I did know she wasn't about to leave me behind. I don't remember what made her scream all those years ago. I can only guess that one of the many unwelcome visitors we occasionally had made her fearful. She was always squeamish toward the occasional bat, moth, or something else that got into our house. But I will have to remember to ask her.

Sometimes my body tells me to move because it senses fear. At other times, I'm paralyzed by it and can't bring myself to move. Every now and again, I have a feeling in the pit of my stomach to be fearful, even though I'm on to something good. Like when I'm getting ready to sign a contract for a new car or home. The possibilities of the unknown pop up in my head and I have this little fear because I'm getting ready to commit several years of my life to paying for it. Thoughts like, *what if I lose my job?* would be rolling around in my head. Or, *maybe I should've chosen the other color. What if the neighborhood turns out to be terrible?* I learn to sort through those guttural feelings and instincts to separate fear from second-guessing.

I try reviewing all the facts from what I uncover while doing my research on such things. It helps me to be confident in my decision, whether the outcome is favorable or not. Some people hear things that sound a bit out of the ordinary and because they can't physically see it, are afraid. It could be a new stock or investment opportunity or a lecture or seminar on technological advances. Fear can either stop you from moving forward or propel you to do so. However you react, you must be able to live with the decision you make no matter how fearful you are in the process.

I sometimes question why so many consumers buy things that can harm them. Afterall, cigarettes can kill you first or secondhand. I'm not here to judge anyone, but I don't put my hand on a hot stove either. I remember a time when there was a smoking and non-smok-

WHY SHOULD YOU CARE?

ing section in restaurants and places of employment. There have always been warnings on each cigarette box or carton. People still have the choice to choose whether to smoke or not, no matter the effects. To think that it is perfectly legal for big companies to sell addictive, cancer-causing cigarettes but illegal for an average Joe to sell marijuana on the streets. When I think about the fact that both are derived from plants and one is known to be more harmful than the other, things don't add up for me. It's puzzling that we have these types of choices, whether or not to consume harmful tobacco products but not harmful ingredients in or on our food.

I don't have a bias on whether a person smokes or not in the comfort of their surroundings. It's their choice. But it does amaze me that certain drugs that used to be frowned upon are suddenly capitalized on by state governments. In regards to marijuana specifically, I feel like it was legalized in certain places to put a monopoly on the profits. Have you ever heard the saying, "If you can't beat them, join them?" There have been many people growing this plant for profit, medicinal, or recreational purposes for many years. Some have even been thrown in jail for having high quantities. It sounds so hypocritical that nowadays wealthy companies with wealthy people can grow and sell large quantities to profit from it and it's perfectly legal in some states. In those states, one has to apply to a state government for a license to sell a product that has historically has already been sold for years. But that alone might not guarantee a green light for business—pun intended. In fact, the license fee alone puts a great number of people out of the marijuana business because they cannot afford the fee. It seems to me certain people are purposefully halted from making money from the plant. In actuality, our government has capitalized and monopolized this arena and told the people, *you cannot but we can*. It scares me how easily this was accepted.

Who can forget the fears of vaccines? How can any employer insist that an employee get vaccinated or lose their job? Does that not violate ones rights? It's a bit unrealistic to me to think that spreading sickness can be eradicated simply on the notion that not everyone wants to be vaccinated. I'm no health expert. Neither am I for or against all the recommended vaccines, but I do believe in choice. Nobody should have to worry about the chatter of vaccines being snuck into the food supply.

It's sad to hear about doctors, nurses, police officers, pilots, and other professional persons walking out of their professions. It's because their natural given right to choose what is put into their bodies has been taken away. There could be other alternatives such as building communities and areas for groups of people who share the same views, like the smoking/non-smoking reference I used above. I'm sure there are other alternative ways we can fit solutions that work cohesively. I think more people should be solution-oriented when it comes to these and other world problems. The sad truth is I don't know what the future of choice will look like, and that unknown could cause many to fear. It's no secret people make rash decisions when they're afraid. I will continue to go with what I know, what I can do to lessen my fears, and hope others will be willing to face their fears for positive change too. But what I find concerning is that there are far few people making decisions for far more without their consent.

My last fear I will discuss is the management of gun safety in our world. If you're a person who has grown up around guns and have used them responsibly, I admire that. I'm not presuming to give an opinion on who should own a gun or not. The concern I have is the large number of guns being produced and the lack of safety measures in place when purchased. There are mass numbers of weapons being sold in the same category of consumer products and goods.

WHY SHOULD YOU CARE?

Why are so many weapons being produced in the first place? Many people are killed each day by gun violence. There are thousands, if not millions, of guns in the hands of people who are getting the guns from unlikely places. Should we be afraid of that? Who do you think supplies them? I wish there were stricter guidelines on the companies that produce guns. Like, how many a company could produce in a given year. It might be helpful if there were limits on the maximum number sold per data per capita. Certainly, many would claim a violation of their rights. But there must be some way to limit guns getting into the hands of those who aren't responsible enough to be safe with them. I often think our gun laws must go further than background checks. Are mental health checks a priority too? Certainly, people have a right to own and carry. What would it look like if every weapon sold came with a locked box for safekeeping? Would accidental child shootings decrease? I don't know. I just know there needs to be a conversation on how we can improve gun safety.

I know I can't come up with a solution to all these fears and other world problems on my own. I only know that we've become a society that is more concerned with offending a group or hurting a group's feelings than stating facts and scientific truths. I don't know how we can unite as countrymen when millions of us have our own ideas of what fear and safety look like. It seems people have made their own decisions on how to protect themselves from certain fears. But fear should drive me and others to try to organize petitions, signatures, and possible solutions for our government leaders to consider taking action on. I don't want my niece, nephew, cousin, friend, or others to be afraid of these and other fears they may have to face. But if they must face them, I hope they're in a place to deal with them with a strong support system and community of people who ask themselves, "Will fear stop me or propel me forward?"

CHARITY PLEASANT

My hopes are that people are propelled forward and not paralyzed by the possibility of shaking a few feathers. The question I have is, how far will our liberties be taken? Why aren't you afraid? I think you should be.

CHAPTER 5

Not Everyone is a Believer

MY MOM USED to play this hand game with my siblings and me when we were kids called bubblegum, bubblegum. It went like this, *Bubblegum, bubblegum in a dish, how many pieces do you wish?* In essence, we would all be sitting or standing in a circle with our two hands forming fists while she rotated tapping our fists to eliminate us one by one until there was a winner. Plus, we got to laugh and play together as a family. I always liked this game because you never knew who was going to win. I always believed I had a chance to win, which some I did and some I didn't. It was always exciting being a part of the competition whether I won or not. But I always believed I had a chance to win. I hope my siblings are as fond of this memory as I am.

Have you ever been in a contest in which you have given the competition all you've got, expecting to get first place only to come in third? Some stop to think, *Wow, third place is pretty good considering the number of people in the competition.* Others may think that they've failed because they didn't win first place. Some even go as far as beating themselves up over it or not congratulating the winning opponent, maybe because they fervently believed they'd win.

Well, I have always managed to see the glass as half full, whereas others see it as half empty. It's because I often think about the flip side of things being worse that it's easy for me to find gratitude. But there are times when it is difficult to stick with my mantras like keeping a positive attitude in the face of not ending up at my goal. Not long ago, I spent several weeks studying for an upcoming test that I really believed that I could pass with no problem. I was so confident that the material was second nature to me. The night before I spent an extra hour going over the material and felt like I was ready.

I set out the morning of and almost arrived late from getting the building location confused. As soon as I arrived, I ran through the ID checkpoint and started the three-hour test—which is a feat all in itself—with confidence. As I began, I clicked through question after question with relative ease. Further in, there was so much more other material on the exam I don't remember refreshing for in my studies, but I felt I should know it either way. After all, I had experience in this subject area. I was watching the time making sure I wasn't spending too much time on the lengthier questions. As my time was dwindling, I began to calculate that there were perhaps more questions on the test than I had time for. So, I hurried through the last few questions, using the process of elimination to whittle down incorrect ones. After I completed the test, I was a little worried about the information I wasn't confident in, but glad the test was over. Two weeks later, I got my results via email, nervously clicking to read my results. I landed four points short of the score I needed to pass this test. Talk about disappointment!

Life is like that sometimes. I had every reason to believe I had the knowledge to pass the test. I certainly had the opportunity to master the subject matter. I prepare for certain events like this and other opportunities for days, weeks, or maybe even longer, only to find that belief alone won't be enough to guarantee my success. I thought that day, *Life isn't fair. How is it that I put in all this effort and sacrifice only to not get the results I was reaching for? How am I not revealing in the rewards of all my dedicated studies?* I could let those momentary feelings deflate my beliefs, but I don't. Life isn't always fair. Belief is only part of the process.

At times, it may take months of effort or longer before I even begin to see any rewards from my due diligence. In other instances, I see the reward of my hard work right away. It's in those times of seeing what I believed manifest that keeps my belief strong. But even if I don't achieve what I'm reaching for now, I believe that things will align for me sooner or later.

Believe me, failing that test did leave me in my feelings for a while. I concluded that life sent my path in a different direction than I had hoped and planned for. But once I overcame those feelings, I chose to believe things would eventually work out for me. Whether re-taking the test will lead me to pass it remains to be seen. Sometimes, there is a lesson to be learned in the hard work and sacrifice alone. I can remind myself that I stuck with something from the beginning, middle, and to the end. The results may not be applied right away, but I can learn from the discipline in the process I have in attempting my goals. I can regroup my methods in hopes to produce favorable results next time.

Not all minds work through unexpected outcomes from the perspectives of believers. A believer trains their mind to adjust. Every day, I try not to focus on the size of my problem. I don't want to magnify them by complaining. I try and focus on the opportunities of solving my problems, and that changes my perception of the problem. I recommend you try it whenever negative responses start to creep into your mind. Believe me, it helps. In my experience, a positive perspective produces a positive attitude, no matter the outcome.

CHAPTER 6

Why Plant Roots in a Place Only Meant to be Temporary?

I LOVE IT when spring rolls around; the tree limbs start to bud, annual flowers return, bright landscaped colors are brought out, and the green grass remerges to signal it's time to get out the lawnmowers once again. I love this time of year when the newness of the season kicks off. I can shed my coat and hat for a while. I see the nursey gardens are starting to open back up again, signaling me to purchase plants and seeds. I see the lush leaves provided by Mother Nature, filling out the trees, providing shade from the forthcoming sun. I love to walk around greenhouses looking at all the variety of plants starting from a little tiny seed. Often, these plants are just barely big enough to be in a small growing container where the seed has started from. But those are not the end place for those plants that started as little, tiny seeds. Seeds aren't meant to stay seeds, just as those tiny fruits and vegetable plants aren't meant to stay plants. They will become food and nourishment for us once they meet the optimal growth and maturity stage and are ready to be harvested.

In the same way, I don't believe we as humans are meant to stay in one place or state of mind. We are meant to grow, learn, evolve, and thrive just as those little seeds and plants do. As I look at some of these plant varieties, I see their roots expanding at the bottom of the planter. I can tell the roots want to stretch out even more. They've reached capacity in their starter container. I believe as humans we reach our capacities in different areas and stages of life. Sometimes we outgrow friendships, jobs or careers, the cars we drive, or the homes we live in. After the plants have grown, they're ready to be transplanted into a bigger pot or a space in the ground where they can expand their roots. Those earlier little pots are just pausing places for the plants; all seeds will soon need more space.

If you leave the plants in their small planters too long, you'll see the roots extending out of whatever opening they can find. Like a confined person who has been limited on what they could do or where they could go for a length of time. Once they find a way out, watch out! This plant example can be used when it feels like you've hit the glass ceiling at work or there's not an inch of space left in your home. There are certain things we need to adjust for in our lives to help us grow, thrive, and reach our full potential.

When I realize that sometimes I ought not to lay roots in spots that should only be temporary, I start to envision the long-term while enjoying the moment. I might not live in the home of my dreams today, but that dream home will be obtained one day. Even the temporary circumstances should be valued. Something as simple as keeping a modest home clean and in order, for instance. Even if you find yourself saving for a bigger home or newer car, try saving a little extra to reach your goal. If you don't mind skipping an expensive cup of coffee or whatever your luxury is every morning to save even more, you'll accelerate the goal. Instead, allow yourself one or two cups per week as a treat so that you can see savings grow. I have found that appreciating the small things makes room for larger ones. When I

WHY SHOULD YOU CARE?

appreciate the subtle movements I make on my journey, like watching the seeds I have planted grow, life somehow moves me closer to my goals and desires.

I've found that some of the goals I have met in life were only steppingstones on my journey. Such as the business I wrote about in my first book that operated four years. I learned a lot from that business about what it takes to maintain one. Many people grow their families, relocate for jobs, and many other reasons that life can change that require people to uproot. As fond as a person may've been about whatever they're leaving behind, it may be harder to leave. Those many seeds that were planted into relationships rooted in community will be missed. But one can take those experiences on to the next planting spot. When I know I have properly laid roots, I'm anchored no matter if for a day or several years.

Inevitably, there comes time for me to get on my knees with my gardening gloves and pull up the ugly weeds starting to grow next to my plants. They're not part of what I planted. They're taking away from the beauty of the other plants. It's funny how life at times works in the same metaphoric way. I often need to pull up the roots of bitterness, unforgiveness, past hurts and pains in my life. I don't want to live in a state of mind of getting back at someone. I just want to pay forward goodness and kindness. Not only that, but each memory good or bad has helped me gain growth and maturity. No need to continue carrying bad experiences into my future. I have to allow new roots to take hold and develop new memories for my future. Putting those old feelings behind me allows me to see the beauty of what is. Say a few words, bury them if I must, and leave them buried. If I don't pull the entire weed from the root, it will reappear. Each time I have old feelings of unfortunate events in my life, I remind myself that those events are a part of my past and that is where I should leave them. Some events leave scars in life that are difficult to ignore. In a way, I see those scars as those annual flowers I mentioned earlier; when you see or feel a scar it's a constant reminder of pain. We all have experienced painful memories. Here is how I deal with the pain I re-encounter in my life:

- Turn off the noise

I turn off all distractions including television, phone, or anything that will disturb me. I get into my bed with a box of tissues and have a cleansing cry. This allows me to really absorb all the feelings I need to for a few minutes, get them out of my system, and feel better immediately. Once I've finished rationalizing all the ways I played a role in the pain as well as how others have contributed to it, I can move on because what's done is done. I cannot go back and change the past, no matter how much I want to. I don't want negative energy taking up space in my heart. I try my best to forgive myself or anyone else who has caused the scars I have. I realize that I can't always get an explanation for why I had to experience the pain, so I try and accept it instead of asking, "Why me?"

- Celebrate

Now is the fun part. I crawl out of bed, turn my favorite music on, and take a shower. If it's too late at night and I fear disturbing anyone, I plug in my earbuds with the music a little louder than necessary and vibe for a while. I listen to my go-to jams that lift my mood. The celebration is a well-deserved one because I was able keep myself from wallowing too long. If I have the opportunity, I might drive to pick up my favorite coffee, snack or meal, or pick up my phone and talk my feelings out to a listening confidant.

WHY SHOULD YOU CARE?

If neither of these are appealing, I have learned to encourage myself. Here are some of the things I say to myself or read.

- I am beautiful – (look in the mirror)
- I am capable – (I can do hard things)
- I am loved – (my family loves me)
- I read my vision board – (I realize some of my visions have become a reality)
- I review the goals I made at the beginning of the year – (I find that I've already accomplished one or some of my goals)

If you're still not encouraged at this point, consider this. I was on a farm recently that grew Christmas trees. The farmer told me from the time the particular tree was planted until harvest time was about six years. The roots of the tree are so vitally important to those trees' survival. They must be able to stand strong winds, crop infestation, extreme heat, cold, or other storms to reach full maturity. The farmer does a little extra anchoring around the trees to support them in the beginning just as we as parents do with our children. But if the trees do manage to survive through those six years of whatever Mother Nature sends their way, many people will have a beautifully decorated tree at Christmas time.

Life to me can be compared to the above in some ways. There isn't much that everyday struggle can do once my mind is determined to thrive. At times, a temporary anchor is all that's needed. A little temporary setback won't sway me left or right, but my mind will tell me to stay the course. Because feeding happens in the root of the plant, it makes the whole plant stronger. That means when I'm fed by the ones encouraging me like family, friends, and others, they're helping me to be strong. When I renew my mind daily with motivation, discipline, and actionable steps that help me stay the course towards my goal, I'm anchoring my roots. There is nothing like a firm foundation amid hardships, struggles, and storms, especially if I remember some of life's experiences are just temporary. So, try these processes when your in the thick of things. I can't guarantee my suggestions will work 100 percent of the time. But I do believe these strategies will help you get through the temporary stopping points in your life. They sure have helped me in mine.

CHAPTER 7

That Phone Call

I REMEMBER AS a teen getting a phone call late one night around 9 p.m. My mom, siblings and I were at our home doing various things around the house when I answered. A friend delivered some devastating news. At the time, we had a phone upstairs on the main floor and downstairs in the basement. Without me knowing, my younger brother was on the downstairs line listening when the call came through. I immediately fell to my knees and broke into tears and screams, my mother looking alarmed as I was completely out of sorts. A few seconds later, my brother rounded the corner from running up the basement stairs in obvious distress too. When we delivered the horrific news, everyone immediately was emotionally torn and crying as well. Someone we knew had been shot. Not only that but inside the building of the church I was born and raised in. I couldn't even fathom that such a thing could happen in a place where I felt so safe, like my second home.

We gathered ourselves and told our mom we had to get to the hospital immediately, not even five miles from where we lived. As shocked as we all were, we arrived at Good Samaritan Hospital where several others had already arrived before we did. As I looked around, many were praying loudly and unashamedly while others were sobbing uncontrollably. As more and more of our church members arrived, leaving standing room only, all we could do was wait. Soon after we arrived, a doctor came where we were waiting to announce that our loved one had passed. They did everything they could but couldn't save them. I was devastated. I knew both the person who was shot and the shooter. I couldn't fathom how such a tragedy could happen to a person so close to me or involve another I was so closely familiar with.

Nobody looks forward to the phone call that comes late or in the middle of the night. It's rare anybody calls with good news during midnight or early morning hours. But when a call comes, one can't help but assume it's bad news. It's never a good feeling, in my mind at least. I immediately start running down the list of possibilities of everything that could be waiting on the other line. I think, *oh, could it be a death? Tragedy? Family emergency?* There is no good way to prepare for that phone call when it happens.

We were supposed to be in church the night of the phone call. I don't remember why we weren't, only that my mother rarely let us miss any services. There must've been a really good reason that we were home during the night we would've ordinarily attended Bible study. In some ways, I'm glad none of us were there to experience what I can only imagine was chaos and trauma for anyone who was in attendance that night.

On the other hand, sometimes I'm sitting by the phone waiting for good news. Impatiently waiting for that phone call to let me know that my loved one or friends are okay. Looking to hear that a flight has landed safely or a surgery has gone very successfully. The time I spend waiting for relief so that my mind will be at ease just slowly ticks away awaiting good news.

WHY SHOULD YOU CARE?

A few years ago, I was waiting for that phone call when a tornado touched down where my mom and two siblings lived in Dayton, Ohio. I had heard the news earlier that day there was a tornado warning but assumed it wouldn't touch down in my little hometown. After all, I hadn't remembered living through a single tornado my whole life growing up in Ohio. Nonetheless, a sibling called me from Dayton and asked if I had heard from our mother and told me a tornado had indeed touched down and they hadn't gotten in touch with her by cell phone since. They'd been trying her several times since it touched down with no answer. The storm did some severe damage in Dayton, including knocking out the power. Another sibling called to tell me they were driving towards our mother's house to confirm she was okay.

While I was sitting up in bed repeatedly calling our mother with no answer, my two siblings were trekking up her dark street on foot with only the light on their cell phones. They told me they had to park their cars on the side of the road at the bottom of the hill because of all the debris blocking access to Mom's street. They were climbing over downed trees, uprooted entirely and flung into the middle of the street, along with siding and other yard items. When they finally reached our mother's house, the electrical lines were down and a huge tree was covering her house and car. Upon reaching her front door and getting inside, she was found safe and sound. Boy, the relief they must've felt to find she was okay because she was tucked away in the basement during the storm.

I don't recall why my siblings' cell phone use was uninterrupted and Mom's wasn't. Maybe her cell tower had been knocked out at that point. But I was certainly put back at ease after that phone call to know she wasn't harmed, and my siblings were looking after her. Thankfully, by daylight, they discovered her house and car weren't severely damaged and neither was she. It's never easy to sit and wait for good news patiently. But when it comes and all is well, it's a feeling like no other.

The tornado did a lot of damage in some areas of Dayton that night. Businesses were destroyed, entire apartment complexes unlivable, homes damaged, and general livelihood came to a standstill while the damage was assessed. It was such a mess throughout neighborhoods and main roads, with many streetlights knocked down, and so much other damage. It took a while for cleanup to be completed and to get back to some sense of normalcy. I have no doubt that those communities will recover. I surely hope many other families had the relief I felt of hearing their loved ones were unharmed. I hope to get more good news phone calls as would anyone else. But when those late at night calls do occur, my breath will almost always catch at the initial sound of the late ring, wondering what will be on the other end.

CHAPTER 8

Shh! Don't Say that!

I GREW UP in an era where you were taught or just knew not to say certain things. Our parents taught us not to address race, sexual orientation, or other life choices that people made. My peers and I were taught not to speak back to an adult, not point out people's insecurities or imperfections, among a laundry list of other things not to say. If when in a grocery store as a child with my mother and I'd noticed someone wearing dirty clothes, if I'd say "Ew! Their clothes are dirty," my mother would grab me by the arm and say, "Shh, don't say that."

In my younger days when I had to compete against someone, I gave it my all win or lose. If I lost, I did not get a trophy. I never once said, "It's not fair." I already knew not to say that. When I got older, I realized that we rarely get what we deserve in life. At times, what we deserve isn't the main point, living life to the full awareness of its beauty is. Even so, if I didn't win that's just the way it was. There was no gloating or making anyone feel bad, and there were no participation ribbons either if one didn't place at least third. Competition in my younger years highlighted those highest achievers at the top of their game.

When I think of some of the things I've heard children say over the past several years, I'm deeply saddened. The vile words that come from mouths of eleven, twelve, and thirteen-year old kids might surprise the average person. But I know that at those ages, many platforms expose them to the words that they say. Because of the many platforms available, it's my responsibility as a parent to take an active role in what my child watches and participates in. Some may call it overprotective, but I just don't believe that children should be privy to adult themes and material unnecessarily, albeit they're not always avoidable.

When I was in my teens, I might've said a few inappropriate things but never around an adult. I knew I would hear, "Shh don't say that." These days it doesn't seem to matter if an adult is nearby, profanity is used by children, inappropriate behavior blatantly happens, and there seems to be no shame about it. I can clearly remember in my teens when I used profanity and felt ashamed of myself for doing so. Even my group of friends would hold each other accountable when one of us were saying a bit too much by saying, "Shh, don't say that." Real friends take the time to explain to their peers why it's not nice to say what was said. I'm always smiling to myself when I hear some children saying that vary phrase to their peers. Those moments fill me with so much hope that not all is lost. Many children are still encouraging really positive actions and I'm happy to get a glimpse of it.

In our politically charged climate today, not too many hold back when they have something to say, no matter who's expense. When I think about some of the derogatory things that are said during elections, I'm disheartened. No matter where you stand, some things just should be left unsaid, in my opinion. People just don't seem to fight fair anymore. It wasn't that there was no airing of people's dirty laundry to try and get an edge on the opponent in my pre-social media days. There was some, but in a no harming type of way.

WHY SHOULD YOU CARE?

As a teen, I was around other peers who campaigned while I attended middle and high school. There were goofy little white lies spread that weren't in the least believable. If things got too out of hand, school administration would take down any offending flyers. When a peer was running for class president or captain of a team, no matter how badly one wanted to win, the process was mostly ethical. Adults can certainly take note here. Some of the ad campaigns during our local and national elections are pitiful to say the least. Someone on the campaign should speak up in these instances and say, "Shh, don't say that" or don't run that.

Like others before me, I have often gotten so mad at myself for something I should've or shouldn't have done. At times, I'd regret that I didn't speak up to tell a friend their actions were wrong. But shouldn't the friend know that already? You'd think that as adults we have the experience of knowing when we were treating someone unfairly or in a biased way. Is it my place to hold them accountable? As a friend I think I should. I have been at fault myself for wanting to prove my point even if it caused unnecessary back and forth. Once the disagreement was over, I've thought to myself, *I shouldn't have said that.*

I would expect a good friend to let me know if I was being unreasonable, overreacting, or overreaching with my words or actions. There are many times I wished I asked a question or said, "Shh don't say that" but I didn't. On rare occasions I wonder if I had only asked one question or made one statement, could the outcome have been any different?

It gets under my skin so much when a person's view doesn't make sense in my head. Not that I urge them to agree with my viewpoint, but to see how selfish or unrealistic their viewpoint is bothers me. But where's my empathy? If two opposing people think they're correct, how is the middle met? Not only does everyone not see in black and white, but there are so many gray areas. Two people won't always have the same truth. It frustrates me to no end when someone tries to continue a moot point. It's during these heated moments I realize how much work I have to do on myself. I've practiced just being quiet in instances that my words, right or wrong, wouldn't improve things.

Have you ever been in a situation where several people are aware that something is going on that is unfair or even wrong? At which point, people kind of look at each other confounded by what to do, but nobody says anything? At times I believe people know that if they say something it may cost them something. I do believe there are people in the room at this time that knows someone should lean in and say, "shh don't say that." It may cause them to be a little less popular or a little less liked. It could lead to being black-balled or whispered about. There are others who know the cost and still decide that they must stand up and say or do something.

Our histories have shown us the people who have been brave enough to speak up and say the things that need to be said. The ones that voiced the things that need to be changed, like Martin Luther King Jr., Georgia O'Keefe, Malcom X, Abraham Lincoln, Billie Holiday, Robert D'Loren, or John F Kennedy, and a wealth of other names familiar and not. Just think about how different our societies would've been if they'd listened to the ones saying "shh, don't say that." It seems that speaking up comes at a cost. The civil rights advocates knew there would be a cost to standing up and voicing that there had to be change in order for inequalities to be heard and taken seriously. Boldness never comes cheap. Some have paid with loss of friends, home, community, or life. There were many women who were the "first" of their times and had to fight for their space in society while

WHY SHOULD YOU CARE?

paving the way for others—to mention a few people: Rosa Parks, Nelam Ganenthiran, or Oprah Winfrey. There are so many movers and shakers today who are continuing to shape our world, improve our quality of life, and make huge strides in humanitarian spaces. It would only take a few clicks of a mouse to discover a wealth of them. It wouldn't be hard to imagine the hardships and perseverance of those who've encountered huge obstacles to achieve what they have accomplished.

I hope that my words reflect that I'm attempting to say what I feel needs said, not only through my perspective but that I can practice what I'm portraying in my daily life. We only have to look at our past to see how much suffering it could cause future generations if things are left uncorrected. When I imagine my son, his future children, and grandchildren, I hope that they will all be brave enough to tell those in their lives, "shh, don't say that" when they feel they should. The ones who speak up anyway are the brave ones who realize their actions come at a cost but still feel compelled to speak out. It is a shame that when people point out something that is harmful to others or would cause wrongdoings, they are called whistle-blowers, demonized in the news, or their livelihoods are turned upside down for exposing the truth.

The truth is—or at least my truth—is that such facts need to be brought to light in order for people to begin to be enlightened and make their own choices. There will always be those who oppose letting the public in on information that may be useful, especially if it will lessen their bottom line. I'm not saying everything is everyone's fight. Only that everyone should advocate for some cause. We must effect change in the ways that we can. Staying silent too long will become commonplace, causing the conscience to scream, "Shh, don't say that." Don't let truths not be said because of how uncomfortable the words will feel. Be proud that you were brave enough to speak out, strengthen your community, or take a chance to change the world when your voice counts the most. People depend on factual information to make more informed decisions. So, whether public or private, remember the liberties we all have came at a price someone else paid. Consider how the words we say are heard by the ones closes to us. Do we want to be proud or remorseful about what we say? I want to be proud, both about the words I choose to speak and the ones left unsaid. It's imperative to understand a negative comment can hurt ones feelings, impact ones confidence, or follow a person for years to come. So, take heed when a friend pokes you discreetly or gives you another sign. They might be saying, "Shh, don't say that."

WHY SHOULD YOU CARE?

CHARITY PLEASANT

WHY SHOULD YOU CARE?

CHARITY PLEASANT

WHY SHOULD YOU CARE?

CHARITY PLEASANT

CHAPTER 9

What Are We Really Doing About This?

THIS IS WHERE the reading may get a little uncomfortable. That's why I saved it for the rear to ensure you'd at least make it this far. I've been in a room a few times in my life when the topic of race is approached. Some of those times, I've been the only person of color in the room. Even if I'm not, I often can feel the sensitivity of the topic in which people attempt to talk about it delicately without offending anyone else. Race in the world has always been at the top of many disputes, wars, and other injustices for reasons I don't understand. When I think about the fact that just about every US application request wants to know what race you are, I always wonder why it's necessary, even though some would say affirmative action. But it has to be deeper than that. Not too many people have approached it smoothly for obvious reasons. I'm going to attempt to start a conversation about it in a way that addresses some facts and misconceptions, cultural trends, and historical data. I also want to point out some thoughts that will cause action-provoking conversations. I'm going to try not to step on any toes while presenting briefly in these next few paragraphs about our world's hot topics and why I feel it's so important to discuss them one more time.

I would've thought that, with all the human-to-human violence documented, seen, or read about, that we would've changed tactics by now as humans. It seems that we are using the same violent procedures repeatedly. Wars and genocides have taken place in our world because of selfishness, greed, ignorance, hate, wealth, and a variety of other reasons. Will there ever be a time when the needs of more are satisfied? More power. More control. More wealth. What are we doing now to deserve the life we enjoy now? Why are some cultures and groups of people judged so harshly? The saying, "a few bad apples spoil the whole bunch," must carry some truth. Would it help if these topics weren't pushed to the forefront of our minds so often? There are so many reminders of such topics embedded in our brains that people often draw their own conclusions. After all, it's hard to move forward while looking back too long.

One could argue who the first group of arrivals to the Americas was or the facts of people already being here. Some argue Leif Erikson, Christopher Columbus, or someone else. But how could any of them be first if others were already there? History tells us many groups of Indigenous people were spread across what we now call the United States before the age of exploration, some historians believe as many as 112 million people, others around 8 million. Some universities support that there may've been more than 500 different tribes speaking just as many different languages. Whatever the number, most can agree because of the many primary sources maintained over the years that there were many people already here upon European arrival. Who can argue with the truth? Truth doesn't need defending. My question is this: why do a vast majority of groups of people throughout history and today continue to fight instead of coexisting with one another peacefully? If this is and has truly been the land of the free, why does it cost so many so much to get here or maintain a desirable life?

WHY SHOULD YOU CARE?

An entry out of Christopher Columbus's diary shows that Indigenous people were described as "well-built handsome bodies, very fine faces, large and very pretty eyes, skin the color of sunburnt peasants, with straight and coarse hair." It's interesting how Europeans described the Indigenous people when they first arrived. The description sounds like the Europeans are intrigued by what they see. Other documented notes show because of language barriers and cultural differences they find this group of people to be inferior to them. Inferior simply because they don't understand the uses of tools the Europeans bring with them, such as some of their weapons.

It makes me wonder why anyone would judge a person solely by the way that they looked, especially their natural appearance. How can any be judged on their lack of understanding something they haven't even seen before? I often think that fear could've played a factor in why so many groups of people have labeled other groups of people in a negative light. Could it be fear of the unknown? Fear of not having enough for everyone to share? Any other number of fears? I'm sure fear of disease played a role, considering some sources claim that as much as 90 percent of the population was wiped out by the diseases spread between the groups. Some were brought to the Americas and the other diseases were already there that had not been experienced by the Europeans. The fact is civilizations have risen and fallen for thousands of years. It's hard for me to understand why more of them couldn't work together to survive in peace rather than to totally disrupt the social system.

I learned about the Mayflower ship with the Pilgrims landing on Plymouth Rock in the 1600s during elementary school. This group of people seemed to have had much more success in coexisting with the others they met after arrival. Differences aside—color included—they were able to help each other survive and thrive by sharing one another's strengths and skills. That's the earliest history lesson I reflect on, one that included "do no harm," and if it did, your own people dished out the punishments. It depicts the Europeans arriving from Europe to the Americas with a dream of a better life. This is the exact thing many people today are doing when they travel to the US from other countries. Emigration isn't new; many people have set out on ships across the ocean, on foot, railways, and other forms in attempts to achieve safer, richer, and fuller lives.

I believe the goal here was that the Pilgrims wanted to exist in peace and prosperity among the others they met when they arrived. Enjoying a place where they could exercise freedom in religion, speech, and natural born rights among others was a priority. The Europeans, with the exchange of ideas with cultures that already existed, would set the precedent for American life as we know it. Accepting the differences in someone's skin, traditions, choices of practices, or culture was just part of society. Is that so hard for us to accomplish now? It doesn't always have to be survival of the fittest. If we focused today on how we can be assets to one another instead, we'd see that our differences don't really matter that greatly.

As we know, prejudices and classism have existed throughout history. The rank of wealth, the social status from birth, where your parents were born, all of these factors affected your place in society. Thank goodness I live in a world today where anyone can build the future that's desired. In other societies, you might've been raised to do the job your parents had. In some earlier societies you couldn't raise yourself from a lower to upper class citizen. Racism or classism wasn't just about black and white as some people in the US focus on today. If you think about racism on a world scale you will find that it's bigger than two colors. The color of the skin was not originally a detail that one looked at in order to have a slave. In the early Roman

WHY SHOULD YOU CARE?

Empire (which lasted about 1000 years) slaves were mostly foreigners. Some children were born into slavery, some were sold into it. The vast majority of Roman slaves differed little from what most Romans looked like. Aside from being a little sun-worn, their appearances were often no different than their masters. Does race really matter?

Empires have known for many years that the more land they controlled, the more wealth they could accumulate. In order to gain said wealth, empires chose to conquer and enslave people. There has always been fighting among people of different geographical locations. The Romans weren't new to trading slaves, either. Some other areas that participated in slavery include Ireland, Scotland, and Eastern European countries. (https://www.britishmuseum.org/exhibitions/nero-man-behind-myth/slavery-ancient-rome)

During the Atlantic Slave Trade (also called the Triangular Trade) there were millions of slaves sent to the Americas to build wealth. I wonder, could the colonists not afford to pay a wage? Or they didn't want to? Could they trade work for land? Why weren't indentured servants used more frequently during that time, like a small plot of land where one could reap a small portion of the harvest or other ideas that could be mutually beneficial for those wanting to come to the Americas? Why has the need to make gains by any means necessary been a way of life throughout history, including the current terrain? I wish people were willing to see another way.

In any case, we must remember in some instances there was trade going on, like weapons, money, manufactured goods, or other things. Some kings were said to believe the people that they sold or traded were beneath them, such as criminals or prisoners of warring tribes. That doesn't make the slave trade right in any way. What a terrible time in our history that was allowed for far too long.

One hundred years after the Emancipation Proclamation, there were still so many injustices happening in the world. I have to wonder if there will ever be a time when all people accept that every human should be treated humanely? Of all the endless work that has been dedicated to equality there are still many inequalities today. Amid the Black Lives Matter or other campaigns/protests, I've often thought about the meaning or intention behind the movement. The titles of some protests only seem to encompass the social injustices of one group of people for that immediate point in time, when in fact there are many of them.

I can recollect learning about many other of groups who have endured atrocities throughout history since Jesus walked the earth as a Jew and before that. It's hard for me to not include everyone in the movement. It's hard not to see how this and other movements can cause divisiveness, because it causes people to have negative thoughts and images in their minds. Instead, the focus should be on positive ways to move forward. Not to take away from what's being brought to people's attention, but we do often leave out several other ethnic groups that have been and still are being affected by injustice worldwide, racial or otherwise. I wonder sometimes if we as a society have learned from the past indignities. Is it possible for us to change our mindsets from how we feel to what we can do? I know for some people it's hard to see forgiveness when all you remember is the pain from an offense. We have so many tools and resources that we must give a try until we find ways to create new historical data, marking leaps and bounds about improvements in our treatment of everyone in the world.

I see the missing component of any movement, march, or protest to be actionable steps to continue to push for change. For example, during any protest, one goal could be to gather signatures of all the people who are a part of the protest. Those signatures could be used to change leadership or legislation, resulting in those signatures being taken to Congress from that event. There are all these thousands of people together at the same time. What is being done aside from yelling, holding signs, and then going home? Surely, protest campaigns get their five minutes of media attention, causing people to take a closer look at an issue. It would be a good time to set up voting registrations, where every person walked away knowing they were properly registered to vote. Participants could also gain more knowledge about the candidate's backgrounds to educate themselves to be more informed. They would be armed with which petitions to support, what candidates to support, or even what organizations they could support in their own cities. Real, tangible things can be done and not just the ideas I've mentioned so far.

Just think about the number of people that could be directly impacted by knowing where their community resources are located. Or how or where to support non-profit organizations in their local community. Maybe even consider making literature available that included potential policy updates and discussions to change laws. I'm certainly not claiming that no event is set up in this way. Only from experiencing the events I've been to; I'd like to see more specific criteria like these included more frequently.

Maybe after an organized event everyone had a to-do-list— opening a bank account with a credit union instead of big banks, supporting local insurance companies instead of big corporations, ways of supporting local farmers, and the list could literally go on—catered to each event. This kind of real commitment begins afterward. Now, if you didn't figure it out in my first book, you should know by now that I love memorable quotes. Bill Clinton said in a speech,

> "Service is a spark to rekindle the spirit of democracy in our age of uncertainty. When it is all said and done, it comes down to three simple questions: What is right? What is wrong? And what are we doing about it?"

Those words are so powerful to me. It would be exciting to see the differences that could made if we stood by those words. It's awesome to exercise our rights by protesting, as well as doing our part for service opportunities. I'm so glad we live in a society that allows us to do so. Are the people in need aware of how to find resources in their communities that are helping with college tuition, utility bills, groceries, mentoring, business funding, financial training, domestic issues, or a wealth of other things? I'm not referring to state or federal lead organizations. I'm speaking of communities of people with more than enough and willing to share. Teaching strategies to obtain wealth and know-how, gathering together by volunteering time, talents, and organizing specifically to give immediate help for the lives that matter. I'm referring to planting community gardens in neighborhoods where fresh fruit and vegetables aren't readily accessible. I'm referring to supporting small businesses every day, not just on special occasions. I'm speaking of encouraging our strong CEOs, CFOs, and other executives of organizations to run for public offices. Many talented leaders in our community would be great in public offices. If our lives truly matter and race does not, our communities matter so our neighborhoods should organize weekly cleanups if needed for the trash on their streets, increasing pride in all neighborhoods. There could be more co-owned kitchens to provide healthy, affordable meals for the busy working family that are made fresh daily. I'm really interested in the meaningful action steps that can be taken once the momentum of various movements die down.

WHY SHOULD YOU CARE?

Without these actionable steps, it makes me think, *I've contributed to the outrage part, now what is being done about it?*

Now more than there's ever been, there are avenues to spread a message. How can we do our part in not spreading misconceptions, negative connotations, and really unhealthy themes about people? I think it's simple; shh, don't say that don't click that, or don't share that. Whenever you encounter something negative, simply refuse to be a part of it. Every culture is a proud people, often sharing and mixing their heritages. The truth is that one cannot characterize a whole group of people by a few interactions. All cultures have traditions and practices that are different from others. I can respect that. Can you? The fact is our history isn't all pretty. We have the ability to affect how our future history is recorded. What do you want it to say? Better yet, what are you willing to do in the face of injustice? We must collectively insist that our similarities be considered more than our differences.

CHAPTER 10

You Again

MY HEART SANK when I heard the news for the second time. Cancer. I didn't have a good feeling going into the new wave of difficulty that would certainly lie ahead. The first time my mother told me she had cancer, I felt that I could help her through fighting it in any way necessary. I knew people who survived it. Still, cancer is one of those words I prefer not to hear from a loved one. While listening to all her options made by her doctors, I started doing some research of my own. I looked up words like chemotherapy, immunotherapy, cancer, and a wealth of other things related to them. I checked out library books on the subject matter, immersing myself in anything I could to learn about this disease and how to fight it. But I can't lie about how hard this news hit me after losing a relative from the disease not quite two years earlier.

The readings that I immersed myself in led me to understand cancer like this: Our body's immune systems are meant to fight off malignant cells—as a matter of fact, if our immune systems are operating correctly, they're meant to fight off any bad cells within our bodies. If the number of bad cells increase in number by multiplying, splitting into two, or grow larger, then they become tumors. Thus, the healthy cells aren't doing their jobs of apoptosis, or cell death. That gives the cancer cells room to reproduce forever, for all intents and purposes, while attacking and destroying the body from within. These bad cells have no respect for any person, they attack every area of the body that they can.

I have never been a fan of the perceived use or misuse of modern medicine, although it has its benefits, I won't argue that. People need life-saving care, whether it be after car accidents, health crises, or other emergencies not planned. I say misuse because so many people misuse medication, apparent by overdoses accidental or otherwise. Our health care system, in my point of view, is more like a sick care system. Some people only seek medical care when they're feeling sick. There are so many hospitals being built in my city that I wonder why there aren't more facilities being built to educate and prevent people from needing them in the first place. There are literally new pills and medications introduced to the marketplace all the time. What if alterations in our environments, our diet, and our lifestyles could improve our health instead?

When I think about health care I think more of prevention or ways that I can prevent certain health ailments from happening. I think about plans to help increase resistance or reverse conditions. I wonder if improving our well-being, mental health, and physical factors can be health care covered too. As with cancer or any disease, I often think of why doctors focus on killing the bad rather than increasing the body's ability to fight with the good. I wonder if many medical schools have been getting it all backward.

During her first bout with the disease, my mother's doctors had first decided to do a surgery that would remove all or as much of the cancer as they could get. Next, after closely considering all the options my mother had, it was decided she would be receiving chemotherapy as a way to treat any possible microscopic cancer left after the surgery. I objected to chemo after doing my research because I understood it as putting poison into the body with a mission to destroy the cancer. Still I supported her by sitting through some of her treatments when I could. She responded to the treatments pretty well initially. It wasn't until her hair started falling out that she began to feel the ramifications of receiving the treatments. My mother had long hair throughout all of my life and most of hers; it was hard for her to lose her hair that she had never in my lifetime once cut. As a licensed cosmetologist, I had trimmed her hair a few times. Even then she worried that I may've removed too much though I assured her I had not. So, it was difficult for me to witness her hair falling out with the simplest touch of the comb or brush.

I did my best to convince her when this whole ordeal was over that she would have her beautiful locks back in no time while trying to help her during the transition of losing them. Even amid all of the grief this caused her, she seemed to be maintaining a level of positivity. I saw her exercising more than ever and keeping a positive spirit throughout. Looking back, it's hard for me to separate if the short moments of despair were mine or hers. I was happy to see her taking walks more than usual, so I joined her on a few of her walks. The few months that went by felt like the longest ever. I was elated when the doctor gave her the all-clear after her last chemo treatment was finished. It had been a long road my siblings and others traveled with her, and we were experiencing such relief from the good news. The cancer was gone.

The following autumn season after her chemo went on like they mostly did. I was relishing in the seeming victory Mom had over the disease. I was able to focus at work and other day-to-day activities better knowing she was back to good health. It was back to business as usual for me, the storm seemed to be over. I called and checked on my mom almost daily and encouraged her to continue healthy eating and exercise habits. I continued to drive over and check in on her more often. I now see I wasn't asking all of the right questions concerning follow-up appointments or other specifics. So, imagine my surprise when after Christmas I got a call from my mom announcing, "The cancer is back." My mind was spinning. How could this be? She just beat it. So soon? *Not you again,* was my immediate thought.

She told me that the cancer had spread to other parts of her body. Those words alarmed me to no end. I knew from the research I did earlier that it's never a good thing when cancer has metastasized or returned so quickly. I can never be sure, but I thought to myself, *is this cancer genetic? Would this have reoccurred no matter how healthy she became?* I came to the conclusion chemotherapy left her body's systems absent of the good cells it needed to rebuild her from the inside. I wondered if there were any left to fight against such an aggressive mutating disease if it returned. I was heartbroken—to say the least—that my mother was faced with this hurdle. Again. How could she possibly muster enough strength to fight this again? I felt the wind knocked out of me, so I couldn't even begin to imagine what she was feeling.

I'm not sure if I'm right or wrong, but there seemed to me to be something that was missed during Mom's first bout with cancer. In hindsight, I don't remember seeing explicit directions on what to do next. However, I could've missed the feeling of an earthquake during this time period. I wasn't focused on how important it is to rebuild the immune system after chemo treatments. There were pamphlets on heart-healthy diets and such. When I thought deeply about the aggressiveness of the treatment, removing the good cells along with

WHY SHOULD YOU CARE?

the bad, I wish in hindsight I would've formed a plan to help heal her inner workings as well as asked more questions. I should've put more thought into her cellular strength. I'm certainly not playing the blame game here. These were just some of the thoughts floating around in my head.

Later, after reading additional literature, I found that after the treatments it would certainly not be a bad idea for anyone to take supplements with high nutritional values. At a minimum to target the body's cells and main systems to rebuild their functions. I'm not saying that additional supplements would guarantee the perfect bill of health, but I'm certain anyone could benefit from a healthier immune system.

After hearing Mom's cancer had returned, my visits became twice weekly along with daily calls, checking in on Mom's health. Even at twice weekly, it didn't seem to be enough. I stayed with her overnight a time or two to be of any help that I could when she needed the extra help. I mulled over the idea of taking a leave of absence from work or moving her into my home an hour and a half away. It didn't make sense logistically to move her so far from her doctors. Her immunotherapy treatments required her to go in on a schedule. I wanted to care for her in a larger capacity. But even if I took a leave of absence, I had my son to get back and forth to school each day. Aside from that, I didn't believe that I could sit 24 hours a day watching her fight a second time around knowing there wasn't much I could do other than love, support, and pray for her. I felt the best I could do was to make the 80-minute drive back and forth when I could, doing what I could while just being with her.

I know that privately some people are fighting battles huge and draining that most others know nothing about. That's why I'm compelled to share my experience with the hopes it will encourage others. You will see that your true strength often shines through in those necessary steps toward whatever tasks that seem insurmountable. I'm so grateful all of my siblings willingly shared the load of caring for her in addition to other relatives, close family, and friends during this very difficult time. Even so, I couldn't believe how quickly she was declining as the weeks went on. There were some relatively good days in a manner of speaking. I will say that it is not my wish that anyone would have to suffer watching a loved one in such a state. One that the only way to keep from tearing up inside is to keep moving and do whatever you can to maintain sanity.

I had to take what was happening with the disease at face value and not have my feelings on my sleeve. I didn't want to show Mom how much I was suffering from seeing her suffer. I couldn't afford to have a breakdown or a good cry, especially not in front of her. So, I held it together outwardly each time I was in her presence, only inside my body was screaming, *You're losing her*. Her body weight was decreasing rapidly with the disease not allowing her to keep food down. The medications kept her sleeping many hours of the day. The medications also caused her some confusion at times which hurt me deeply. The one thing I could never forget is that her faith in God stayed strong, never once swaying.

In the beginning of Mom's second bout of the disease, each time I prayed for her, and I prayed a lot, I'd ask God to heal her. I was quoting scriptures to myself and God, using motivational teachings and songs for encouragement, Bible story reminders, and anything else I could soak up to keep both her and I believing God was able to do anything. Somewhere along the way my prayers changed to, *God? Comfort and be with her.* It's amazing that at times the spirit guides me how to pray.

WHY SHOULD YOU CARE?

Throughout my life I've experienced that prayer can certainly change things and situations. Other times, prayer sustains me or changes me instead of my situation. Sometimes immediate change isn't the case. Before this test, I'd experienced month after month of praying for the same thing only to face the same ordeal. Even though I know I can't, I try and find why God doesn't deliver me from the ordeals. It's hard for me to accept that prayer doesn't always change the *will* of God. I have to accept I won't understand his will at the same time believing he not only knows best but indeed has a purpose for his plans. Even with all my faith I was watching Mom become physically weaker each time I saw her, but her faith never swayed. The discernment in my spirit led me to pray for his will to be done.

Observing how things were progressing had me second-guessing myself. I couldn't determine if I wasn't sacrificing enough, perhaps I wasn't praying enough, some sin of mine was blocking me from reaching God, or if my spirit was already telling me, "It is well with my soul." There seemed to be a type of preparation in my heart that God was doing. In many other difficult situations, I would not have thought twice about rejecting what we were facing. I would've insisted that it couldn't be possible. I didn't just give up, I attempted to find ways to lift her spirits when I could, make recommendations for herbal supplements, and at least sit in on some of the care conversations with her care providers. All the while, I tried to listen to what Mom wanted too. I didn't always agree on what the doctors discussed with her, and I voiced it loudly. I objected to some of the suggestions outright. I had to listen to my mother's point of view and think about the way she understood things. She was raised during an era when people put a lot of trust in what their doctors prescribed. I, on the other hand, question everything. She was fighting in her own way with prayer and exercising her faith. I could see that plainly.

I have heard people say phrases like, "Why me?" or "What have I done to deserve this?" The most popular one I think of is, "God won't put more on you than you can bear." So, I think to myself, *What do I get out of this whole experience? Why does God think I can bare this? Why does God think she can bear this?* Life is beautiful. Life is precious. This I know. But what I really absorb and take away will indeed follow me for the rest of my life. You see, my mother passed away, and I, along with all my siblings and sibling in-laws, had the honor and privilege of being in the room with her when she transitioned from this life to the next one. She fought all the way up to her last minute. She loved me, her other children, family, friends, and she considered us all the way to her last minute here. Those last few weeks watching her battle cancer allowed me to see how strong my mother truly was. She was indeed a fighter, something that I see clearly that she passed on to me.

She showed me each day of her struggle how strong her faith in God was. She said things like, "God is in control." She prayed and called to her God up until the last moments she had with us. I heard her repeatedly thanking God each day, even during her sleep. I can't begin to try and describe the experience of seeing life leave a loved one. I can say that she was here one moment and gone the next. There were those dual feelings appearing again except this time they felt both beautiful and terrible. Beautiful in the sense that I could be there with her and terrible in the fact of seeing her go.

I could not bring myself to leave her, so I sat next to her for a long while after her transition, taking in her beauty and strength, talking to her, and holding her hand. I cried as my heart was overwhelmed with anger, guilt, love, and sadness but still some understanding. I was trying to process all that had happened over the last few weeks and months. Was there something I missed or could've done differently to extend her time or ease her pain? I thought to myself that I really dropped the ball. I should've been even more involved in her care. I should've spent more time with her. I should've refused some of the suggested treatments. I should've taken her home. I should've taken a leave of absence from work. It was difficult to process all of the thoughts going on in my mind. I had to keep reminding myself that I am not God. It was hard to bring myself to leave my mother as my siblings made arrangements for her. After how long I couldn't say because time might as well had stopped, I finally said my goodbye. I kissed her already cool and stiffening body, I held her hand one last time and tried to make my peace. I cried again, not wanting to leave her alone as we departed and left the hospital and funeral home to do their part. I accepted that she was gone although I still could not believe it. Somehow, as unfair as it felt, I had to continue life without my mother dearest.

It seemed unfathomable that I had to go to sleep at night and wake up each morning with the same reality that my mother was gone. It took a few months for me to accept that I could not reach for the phone to call her and share my good or bad news. The urges I feel are happening less often. But I often imagine what she'd say if she heard it anyway. I have loved my mother my whole life and still love her even though she's not physically here with me. Some days when I see her picture in my home, I look at it and say, "I love you, Mom." It doesn't weird me out to see her picture daily or to be in her old room when I visit her house. Although I just can't seem to get used to her being gone. At times, while laying down to sleep at night, I think about her and the months leading to her passing. I'm not sure if this is grief, regret, guilt, normal or abnormal, or any number of other things. But during those nights I wrestle with I could've, would've, and should've. I know that there are things that are beyond my control. I keep coming to the same conclusion even after my mind races in a thousand directions and the tears just won't stop: "It is well." No one in life is immune from pain or death. I have to let God be God.

I somehow am so confident in all the ways I showed her I loved her. Mom's fight showed me how desperately she didn't want to leave us. The evidence of my love was shown here, there, and everywhere over the years. As an adult and mother, I truly understood the strength of a mother's love. It became clear to me how fiercely Mom loved me both as a child and adult. I'm confident my mother knew how much I'd always love her as well. Recently, I came across some very dear writings that I'd given my mother over the years and thought I was indeed an expressive love giver and possibly a writer in the making. I wrote a couple of poems and letters for her for encouragement. Although I cannot remember how old I was, I showed my mother I loved and appreciated her. I believe these two writings to be in my late teens and/or early twenties. I'm sure they were to encourage her that although I gave her great struggles with my behavior early on, I indeed loved her, too. (See earlier works in Appendix section at the back of this book.)

It has been difficult not being able to talk to the person who phoned me almost daily and knew and understood me more than anyone on earth. I take solace that my mother loved me more than her heart allowed, and that she's resting, experiencing no more pain, with her soul at peace. I will try my best to continue her faith and legacy of love. Every now and again I accomplish something like finishing this second manuscript of mine and think she would be proud. Sometimes I see one of my mom's favorite foods, but I cannot bring myself to eat it. Even though I can still hear her saying, "Treat yourself and watch a movie." Mom always wanted me to relax and do things for myself. I know I have a similar heart to hers that loves to serve others. That's one of the reasons I rarely slow down. I'm sure I

WHY SHOULD YOU CARE?

will face life's hardships, sickness, or any other low blows of life once, twice, or even three times or more on the rest of my journey. I will try and get through them with the level of faith, hope, and love that my mother taught me, even though in the back of my mind I know it would be impossible to match her level of faith and dedication to God, community, and family. But I will continue to remember what she demonstrated by not saying a word. Her life said it for her. I'll just reflect that—the legacy she left behind.

CHAPTER 11

How to Move from Test to Testimony

I REMEMBER ABOUT eight or nine years ago; I was working a second shift job from 2 to 10:30 p.m. During that time, I was newly separated and in the middle of dissolving my marriage. My son was young, about five or six years old. He'd just started kindergarten. I would get him ready every morning, drop him off at school, and by the time I got off work, he was fast asleep. I struggled with the fact that the only waking hours I spent with him in a day were those two hours in the morning getting him ready for school. Aside from that, I didn't spend waking time with him until the weekends. I liked my job but couldn't rationalize the worth of continuing it if it minimized my time with my son. I struggled with whether I should start a job search again elsewhere or look within the organization for more conducive hours. After contemplating this decision for several days, I sprang into action. I scheduled an appointment to talk with my boss to let her know my concerns. I nervously finished sharing my dilemma and braced for how she would respond. Without hesitation, she said she had the perfect job for the hours that met my needs. As she explained the details, I listened intently.

Next, she looked at me and asked, "Can you start next week?" At that moment, I realized that my work ethic had resulted in such a good reputation that she was confident that I would carry those same ethics into another position. In my job duties, I tried to do a little more than what was expected of my tasks with a smile. I was dependable, on-time, had nearly perfect attendance, and worked well with people. She told me she'd received repeated emails about how well I represented the organization as well as how thoroughly I completed my tasks. I'm not trying to toot my own horn but show how important it is to maintain a quality work ethic. To my surprise and elation, I started quite quickly in the following week, just as she asked. That's what I call my testimony. I moved from my test to testimony by first admitting I was struggling with my current hours, devising a favorable plan, and not faltering in my performance while putting my plans into action.

Often in life I go through tests, trials, and struggles, just as countless others do. At times, they are longer than necessary simply because I do not ask for what I want or need because I assume I have to suffer through it. At other times I don't seek change because my mind tries to reason me out of it. I think that it will be risky, uncomfortable to ask for help, that the new environment could be worse than the current one, or it may be unattainable. Sometimes, it's all about asking the right questions or taking a leap of faith. During those times, it's important to me to remember that what I go through can be used to build my character. Sharing to help others who may experience similar predicaments is also important to me. If while amid of my test I only think about the test, I often miss the opportunity of my growth and my testimony. Strength, resilience, and confidence are built when I move from test to testimony. Every test, trial, or struggle increases my knowledge of what matters. After I emerge on the other side of them, I realize I'm stronger than I thought I was. Aside from that I learn patience, how to appreciate the moment, how to be resourceful, rely on hope, and action. In my above expe-

WHY SHOULD YOU CARE?

rience I could've easily moped around, worked half-heartedly, felt sorry for myself, or complained every day. Instead, I moved from problem to solution. Here are my actionable steps to move from test to testimony:

- Admit I'm struggling
- Pray – Seek wisdom and guidance
- Brainstorm – Write down possible solutions
- Plan – Prepare actionable steps that guide me towards my goal
- Believe – Believe experiencing the test is building my character
- Positive attitude – No matter how grim, positivity changes my outlook
- Act – Start what I have planned in faith
- Be Grateful – Life is beautiful; my struggles build strength
- Wait – Watch for the goal to be met because of the steps above

You may have a similar actionable process or strategy or you may do something completely different. Whatever it looks like, remember however deep or dark the test or struggle may be, you'll eventually end up with a testimony. The result may not happen as quickly as mine did. But I don't always get fast reprieve either. Life can often weigh me down with stress. You'd think that I'd be used to life's stressors by now. But every now and again I go, "Wow, I don't know if I can do this." When I run into these stressful times that hit me totally unexpectedly no matter how much I could've planned for them, I go into the mode I described above. When the above actions don't seem to be enough, I follow the steps below. Without fail it helps me when the struggles are real.

When I'm struggling with life, I use what I read in a quote by Saint Francis of Assisi. "Start by doing what is necessary, then what is possible, and suddenly you are doing the impossible."

First, I begin by doing only the necessary things. How does one define that? Necessary may be putting my feet over the edge of the bed, down onto the floor, and simply standing up. Once I have done a few of the necessary things, I continue by doing the possible things I think I can get through. How does this look? The possible may be cooking my child breakfast, packing his lunch, and getting us out of the door for school. In my case, I drive my son to school every morning, so getting out of bed is a must even when I don't feel like it. For some, doing all that may be enough to make them crawl back into bed. But if for just a moment one thinks about all that was accomplished this far, before you know it, you'll look up and notice you have completed what you once thought was impossible.

Because this process at times works for me, I encourage you to keep going. So instead of getting back into bed and pulling the covers up over your head, turn on some catchy music, clean the kitchen, take a shower, and drink a cup of coffee or tea. You may find the energy to do other things you thought were impossible. You might find joy in realizing what you've accomplished. That joy just might spark the long-term change you so desperately needed. Every one of those tasks and others I didn't mention may've been painful to get through. Surely you feel the joy as well. If you can just start with a little belief in yourself, it may take you further than you originally imagined. Try and pull a positive nugget of wisdom out of all life's tests. You might be surprised how your testimony is used or who it impacts in a positive way.

We spend so much time planning, reaching, or building that we often miss being in the moment. When we're in the moment, we give attention to the people around us. We make those we love a priority. That means ourselves too. If we're taking time to absorb the day-to-day, we stay in-tuned to others' feelings and emotions. We can often be in tune with nature and the beauty of it. Often, I can tell when something unusual is going on with a friend, relative, or co-worker without them saying a word to me because I'm in-tune with them. So, take a few minutes to check on someone you love. Maybe try listening even if it's hard. You never can get past the surface of people if you don't let them know you truly care. So, when the time comes and you are tested, remember where you were, how far you've come, and envision where you want to be. If you're in the test now, try to focus on the testimony that will be. Even if it lasts a while you'll likely interact with someone who just made it out of theirs. A positive attitude may not change the situation. I believe it might change you or the way you see the situation.

CHAPTER 12

My True Love is Entrepreneurship

IF YOU'VE READ my first book, then you already know about my business experience owning a hair salon and my time owning multiple properties as a landlord. My love for anything business started all the way back when I first started earning money baking cookies that I got my dad hooked on. When I saw that he couldn't resist them, I continued to bake them weekly or bi-weekly, not knowing at the time I was learning about supply and demand. Starting around twelve years old and continuing into high school, I began servicing hair clients for every time and season.

During these last few years, I have been able to hold a traditional place of employment while keeping my entrepreneurial skills polished and ready. My love for business, both profit and non-profit, has led me to many connections throughout my community. My calling for business has been intertwined with service, too. I believe what I read from a prominent entrepreneur who said, "If you want to get more, you have to give more." So, I've managed to give my time and talents along the way of building connections. I'm always inspired by people and experiences that I encounter throughout my journey.

Several facets about entrepreneurship keep me mesmerized. First, the unlimited potential there is for building a brand that one can be proud of. When someone hears about or researches "Pleasant Investments LLC," I want the brand to speak for itself. I know that I haven't arrived there yet. But the great thing about that is that I can navigate where I want it to go. To have some control over the mission and goals of my products or services brings such gratification. I say some control loosely because as an entrepreneur I understand that a person operates solely or with an entire team. I also like the earning potential possible depending on how much time and effort one is willing to put in.

Another aspect I love is that I can see the finished results of a product or service. It's different when the process is experienced up close from beginning to end and you know you had a part in it. I love being a part of the development, and including my input fills me with so much pride. There's so much more pride in the process when I have a part in it. There's even joy for me when I learn about others being successful in their businesses and aspirations. I have several family members who have been entrepreneurs in their communities. It makes me proud to see their achievements.

A business mindset has given me the ability to see the world and all that is happening in such a way that I believe makes opportunities and resources more noticeable. I can't say that I know what most people are thinking, but I can say that I see what some people are doing. The actions I see going on around me, or lack of action, give me ideas to excel in my areas of strength.

I recently set out on a trip that I will call "across the country." I drove from Ohio to Nevada, which is the furthest I've driven solo to date—yes, that's across seven states—in order to pursue a service opportu-

WHY SHOULD YOU CARE?

nity with the AmeriCorps organization that would allow me to see the countryside simultaneously. I can't say that I wasn't a little nervous or that some of my friends and family didn't think I was a bit crazy. But I only had to have the confidence to set out and begin. It turned out to be a great adventure. I drove each day until I was tired or it was dark. Whenever I felt like stretching my legs or a restroom break was needed, I simply pulled off the freeway on an exit with attractions.

Some would call it a stroke of luck that on one of my leg-stretching stops I ended up at the Danish museum in Iowa. There the museum was featuring a multi-talented artist who happened to be inside and I was able to meet her and her husband. They were a lovely couple, both talented in their own rights. I had the chance to share with them a copy of my book. I met some awesome people during my Nevada stay and had fun exploring the state while doing so. That is why I'm so willing to share my experiences and connect with like-minded people. I'm never afraid to share exactly what I know that may help the next person.

I believe entrepreneurs should pay close attention to a variety of things, whether they're interested in them or not. There are some key things that I recommend you do no matter what business you are in. One–pay attention to trends so that you can reinvent yourself or your business as needed. For example, more people are using social media than ever before. So, it would make sense to keep business websites up to date with different ways for the customer to stay engaged. If including links to other media platforms or newsletters is what works, include those. If you find not many people are opening your newsletters, try another tactic.

Two–if you have multiple products or services where one product is significantly outselling another product or service, it might make sense to put more marketing energy into that popular item or service. Mabey even let the less performing product or service fade out altogether or offer it by request only. If you can afford to give something away with referrals, do so if the referral results in a purchased amount covered by the item or service you can give away. It could even be something like a free literature pamphlet with recipes, some helpful links, or coupons for additional purchases.

Three—don't object too fast to volunteer opportunities or giving a product or service away. Although your goal is to make a profit for your business, there is a lot to be said about volunteering a small amount of your time or giving a product away and gaining a huge benefit from doing so. Not too long ago, I donated two free copies of my books to an organization that resulted in a purchase order of 50 of my books. The two giveaways generated much more additional sales.

The fourth thing I highly recommend is to set aside a monthly budget for your business. I made the mistake early on during my first self-published book by not having enough set aside for taxes or to invest in myself. Your business livelihood depends on advertising, which can include joining a club pertaining to your business. This will help you get into the minds of people with the same needs as you. Although some may require an annual fee, the right one will prove worth it. You will also find local events in your area where you can be a vendor or send someone out to represent your company. This will help your local community see who you are so people can spread the word for you. Believe me, other opportunities will come up, and you need to be prepared to pay for them.

Five—never stop learning about your craft, how the laws are changing, and how they might affect you and your business. You may be

WHY SHOULD YOU CARE?

an expert in your business, but the fact is that business methods are always changing and so are the laws. I always am in a bit of a rush at the end of the bi-annual year because I need to renew my cosmetology license in time before it expires. The Ohio State board usually requires that I take a minimum number of classes in order to fulfill the CE hours I need to renew. But the year after Covid those rules were altered so it benefited that I paid attention to them. Regardless of the laws, I always continue to educate myself by going to at least one industry show to see what is new and popular and take advantage of sitting through several classes in one weekend. Even if I don't utilize all that is new, I may find something I want to incorporate immediately.

I could say so much more, but there are thousands of books on business. I'm sure you can educate yourself in that subject area successfully. Make sure you surround yourself with people who are smarter than you. If you are always the smartest person in the room you are in, you're not learning, growing, or pushing yourself to become all that you can be. So don't worry about if they happen to be younger than you are. Get over that. Having a younger person means they can reach a younger audience in ways that you might not be able to. More importantly, you need to find people that you can trust to handle business needs when you're vacationing or unable to do so. Burnout is real. You need to rest easy knowing you left someone in charge that you trust while you get some rest and relaxation. Those people will become vital to help you grow your business. It will help that you have someone who is smarter at an aspect of your business that you may consider to be boring or simply uninteresting. Even though you may run your business solo, there may still be certain aspects that you just shouldn't do. Take my writing: although I consider it to be my craft, I would be remiss to not have an editor review my manuscript and critique it before I publish. The editor is way more qualified to do so. You might not enjoy the same entrepreneurship paths that I follow, but if you're just starting out, make sure you have plenty of support and I believe you will be successful.

CHAPTER 13

Life Is But a Dream

SOME OF MY dreams are so vivid that I actually wake up screaming. I'm falling from such a high altitude that even once I've awakened, it feels like I'm still falling. Or I'm being attacked by a swarm of bumblebees, so I wake up twitching and swatting at the air in front of me. Once I can stop my legs or arms from moving, I have to work on slowing down my heart rate. Some of my nightmares are so devastating that I often wake up in tears from the realistic feeling it leaves because of the possibility of the nightmares actually happening. I also have really good dreams that overtake me during sleep at night that I don't want to wake up from. During those moments, I try to will myself back to sleep to enjoy a few more minutes of the beautiful haze. Especially ones like how millions of dollars would change my life.

There have been many people who have been credited with telling people what their dreams and nightmares mean. One of the most famous was Daniel to King Nebuchadnezzar. I can't help but wonder if mine are premonitions or fantasy. I've heard people say that eating certain foods before bedtime may cause some dreams to be more vivid than others. I've heard it said that tryptophan is produced by a certain vitamin that trips serotonin levels in your body which contributes to vivid dreams. Could some spiritual power be trying to get my attention at times to open my awareness to guide me toward or away from harm or danger? The truth is I don't know. On occasion, I know I have watched too many science-fiction movies that day which gives my brain ideas as I lay down at night. At other times I lay in bed and my mind just takes off so fast in so many different directions, giving me so many ideas that I need to get up and write them down.

My dreams could be more than just extended thoughts and imaginings too. I dream of achieving goals, enhancing the lives of others, and visiting many places I haven't seen. The best thing about those dreams is seeing them fulfilled when I'm awake by the choices I make in life. It's even exciting when those dreams aren't achieved yet because I know I have something to look forward to. On other nights my dreams are just dreams, completely fictional in nature. Boy, can they be outlandishly creative! Some of the dreams that I have when I'm vividly reliving my past surprise me. When I wake, I think to myself that maybe I haven't quite let the past completely go hence the re-occurrences harboring my peaceful night's sleep.

Those dreams of my past experiences with people I know cause me to remember my life's few regrets. I find myself waking up wishing I had changed how I acted or reacted to a past challenge or experience. I try in those cases to make a mental note and get back to sleep. Sometimes my mind makes up challenges and plays them out in my dreams in the ways I think I should act or react if faced with a specific challenge. Is there something I still need to learn from my short history here? Is there something I still need to say or do? Learning for me—I hope—will never end. I feel there are tasks still for me to complete. But isn't life indeed a dream? We all have a short time being here on earth to live, thrive, connect, love, soar, learn, and so much more.

WHY SHOULD YOU CARE?

There are other days when I feel like I'm walking around in a dreamlike haze. I'm going through the motions of tasks and details I need to complete without feeling in touch with myself at all. I'm getting out of bed, driving to work and returning home, only to feel as though I didn't feel anything all day. I don't always have time to think about how I feel because if I do then I cannot focus on what I need to accomplish. In my own way I sometimes allow the fogginess to be a distraction. In that seemingly short time, I don't have the patience to deal with the reason I'm in the daze. In those moments, I've realized it's because I'm doing what I think I have to do, not what I actually want to do.

I know I need to listen to my feelings, process them, and pay attention to what my mind and body are telling me. Lately, my thoughts and dreams are focused toward living my life in abundance coupled with all the skills and knowledge I've gained. I want to ensure I attract the abundance that I want. I want to speak positively about my life and future dreams. I will no longer allow negative thoughts to fester. I will be aware that they pop up so that I don't give them too much attention.

I remind myself that my thoughts, feelings, and emotions need to be dealt with. Only I know that I have always dealt with my emotions differently from others. I don't let people see what I'm feeling, what I dream of accomplishing, or much else of my goals. I feel at times I can't let everyone in on what I'm dreaming because they may not bring good vibes. Sometimes I'm not sure how those dreams will become a reality. In a way, I think if I say them out loud then I will have to follow through on what I've said. Other times, when I say them aloud, I believe I'm willing them into existence.

On other days, I'm not dreaming at all. I've learned to appreciate the nights when I awake and can't remember dreaming about anything.

I think those are the nights my mind actually gets the most rest. But those are just a few fleeting moments. I wonder if some people dream more than others. I wonder what it says about a person who does or doesn't dream. But I know I dreamed of finishing this second manuscript and here I am towards the end of my book. Hopefully, you've made it here with me.

When I sit and daydream about love, hate, and other things, I hope I dream more of love and my talents I will use more often. I find that when I'm doing the things I love and want to do, everything else falls into place. When I dream of a more perfect system, I dream of all the ways our laws could be rewritten, and our leaders being invested in a moral high ground. When I dream about the possibility of another pandemic in my lifetime, I don't let that fear of what I've experienced stop me from progressing forward. But you will never hear me say that I'm not afraid. The truth is, at times I'm scared to death I'm running in the opposite direction I'm supposed to be going. I'm nervous that I'm making important decisions too hastily or too slowly. I'm not always clear if the decision I made was a good one or not. That's where I have to believe the fear itself is temporary, it only exists until I conquer it. When I do, those fears turn into testimonies. So the next time someone tells me, "Shh, don't say that don't dream that" I'll respond with, "Not you again." I've had that phone call before. I must be dreaming because I've seen this play out before.

Expressing my thoughts through words has been so much more gratifying than I originally dreamed it would be. When I think about which thoughts and ideas I was exposed to growing up were the most important, I come to a quick conclusion. There were very many. Religion, good financial and eating habits, following the rules, developing into a good citizen, positive representation of myself and my family—all these were among the top. My parents never insisted I get

WHY SHOULD YOU CARE?

straight A's in school, take advanced math or science, go to college, get a high paying job, or experience other countries. But they taught me lessons I cannot forget. My father continues to teach me to really see what is going on in our world today and how to be a part of the truth. My mother left me a heart of service and love for everyone and everything. They both instilled in me to be the person who did the things I said I would do. I'm not even sure if they knew. The wisdom and enlightenment I received from my parents mostly came from me watching them live. I can only dream that this reality right now will cement my purpose because I'm doing the very thing I want to be doing. I want to continue so much more because the paths that I have taken so far have brought me here.

I've learned to be grateful for what I have instead of what I don't. I'm thankful for those who support me instead of bad mouthing those who don't. I appreciate today instead of thinking about what happened or didn't happen yesterday. I look forward to tomorrow, no matter what life brings. A new day may just be the brink of something new and wonderful happening. So, I do my best to love now, laugh now, pray now, and live now because there will never be another opportunity like the present one. I've found that the key to experiencing life is to just live it. Life tends to pave the way for those who start today instead of planning for tomorrow. Go ahead and start living to the fullest today so you won't have to look back and ask, *was this all just a dream?*

Appendix

My Dear Mother

We have been mother and daughter since June 9, 1980. For as long as I can remember, we have had our ups and downs. But through that, I have learned the way to the top is from the bottom. It is you who taught me to be an independent woman. You have also taught me what true love between people really is. I have watched you sacrifice through long, hard working days only to return home unappreciated. I've slept while you were out working all night, returning home each morning with no one to rub your feet. I've watched you go to church day in and day out with a love for God I've never seen or understood until you. I've watched you make one sacrifice after another so your children had a place to lie and food to eat. I only wish you knew how much more you deserved then and now. I look back over my life at all the tests and trials I've been through and thank God for them all. It is those tests and trials that made me the strong, beautiful, Holy Ghost filled woman I am today. I want you to know that I thank you for all your prayers you prayed for me, even when I wasn't mindful of the junk I was getting into. I want you to know I appreciate you each and every day, my dear mother. I want you to know even though those whippings hurt, I needed them. I want you to know you have instilled in me morals, values, respect and so many more good things. I want you to know you could have given up on me, but because you didn't, I found a way within myself to prove to you I would be O.K. And most of all, I want you to know that all of the sacrifices you have made for me have been very well worth it. If you can't tell, take a look at me and see what you have made. I love you thoroughly and exclusively, my dear Mother.

Your Daughter, Charity

WHY SHOULD YOU CARE?

According to the CDC, in the US in 2019, 1,752,735 new cancer cases were reported. 599,589 people died of cancer. 2019 is the latest year for which incidence data are available. Numbers below are per 100,000 people. See the data chart below:

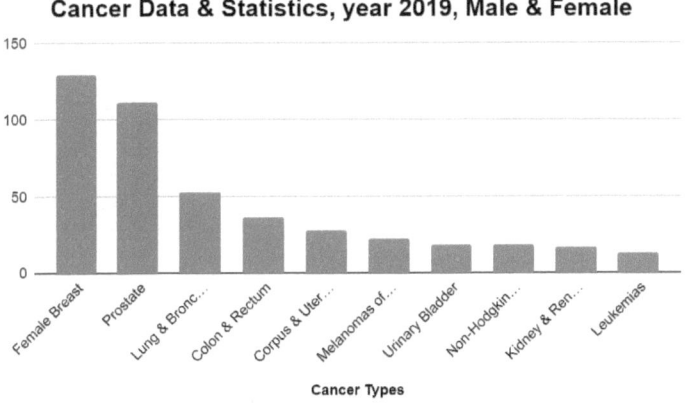

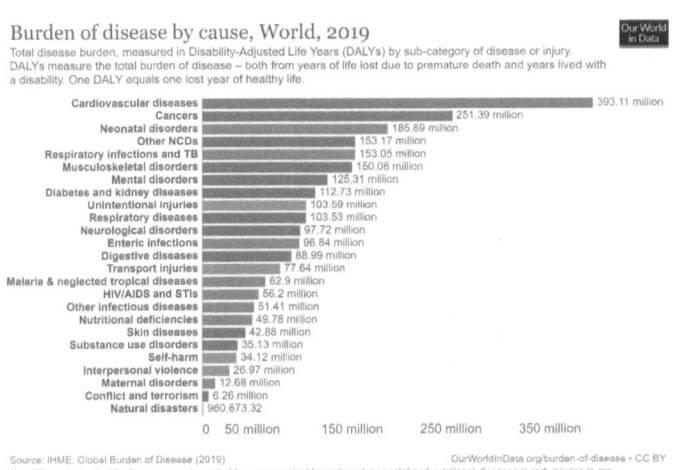

| Data published by | Global Burden of Disease Collaborative Network. Global Burden of Disease Study 2019 (GBD 2019) Results. Seattle, United States: Institute for Health Metrics and Evaluation (IHME), 2021. |

Additional Resources Page

If you or someone you love may be dealing with cancer or other illnesses, these web sites might help in some alternative treatments:

https://www.mskcc.org/cancer-care/diagnosis-treatment/symptom-management/integrative-medicine/herbs

https://www.mskcc.org/cancer-care/diagnosis-treatment/symptom-management/integrative-medicine/herbs/search

https://www.mskcc.org/cancer-care/diagnosis-treatment/symptom-management/integrative-medicine/herbs/herbs-botanicals-other-products-faqs

Category - ALL OUR PRODUCTS (king-cart.com)

Recommended Book

The Truth about Cancer: What You Need to Know about Cancer's History, Treatment, and Prevention Ty M. Bollinger

A few of my favorite things

Lois Deals
Tool & Supply wholesales based in Georgia

G-Stringz (music)
"Get To Know You" on YouTube

DJ Loki of The RedZone DJs
www.theredzonedjs.com

The Mims Company
The Mims Company, LTD

The Whole Woman's Homeopathy

All The Things That Nobody Told Me: Finding the Extraordinary in My Journey Charity Pleasant

SM BODY CARE
Products – SM BODY CARE

Author Contacts and Resources

Send a message or request:

Pleasantinvestments123@gmail.com

Make a donation to give a book away:

Cash App – $Charity66

PayPal - Pleasant Investment (https://www.paypal.com/donate/?hosted_button_id=99AGKNRX7JCL2)

Venmo – Pleasant Investments

Purchase hair products at my online hair store through Salon Interactive:

https://shop.saloninteractive.com/store/PleasantInvestmentsllc?utm_source=SalonInteractive&utm_medium=web&utm_campaign=ShareMyStore

www.ingramcontent.com/pod-product-compliance
Lightning Source LLC
Chambersburg PA
CBHW060615080526
44585CB00013B/846